Linda Heavner Gerald

# CLAIRE'S HOUSE

East Baton Rouge Parish Library
Baton Rouge, Louisiana

Text copyright © 2016 Linda Heavner Gerald

ISBN-13: 978-1533536624    ISBN-10:    1533536627

Large print edition

# ACKNOWLEDGEMENTS

Thank you David Ryan Tilley for your editorial services.

Ashley Baumann: Many thanks for another great cover.

The author photo is by Debbie Hooper. Thank you.

Thanks to George and Jo Erhart for suggestions on the French.

Ramsey's Printing: Thank you for all of your help.

# BOOKS BY LINDA HEAVNER GERALD

Beaufort Betrayal
Rosemary Beach
Will He?
Dusty the Island Dog
Till Heaven Then Forever
Confessions of an Assassin
Sins of Summer
Murdered Twice
I am Red
Enchanted


Lime Pie Publisher
Port St. Joe, Florida 32457
850-340-1812

# DEDICATION

This book is proudly dedicated to Douglas May.
A young man who endured terrible pain both physically and mentally. Our community watched in horror. We were unable to offer much assistance. His family bravely stood by his side with great faith in God and love for each other. You have blessed us all.

# ONE: CHRISTOPHE & CLAIRE GAUTIeR

Deep in a haunting bayou of Louisiana, a strange plot of enchanting land exists. Beautiful, green grass covers a square plot of two acres. The Gautier family owned two hundred and twenty acres of the land that encompassed this unique piece of earth. Surrounded by massive swamps, the savageness of the area abounds in the folklore from earlier generations concerning this isolated place. Alligators roam as well as large lizards and snakes. Still, the square of land is lovely to behold. A magnetism exists here unlike any other land in Louisiana or the world.
Christophe and Claire Gautier inherited it from Christophe's Cajun uncle, Louie. Claire felt hesitant even to consider building a home on such a raw piece of land, but her husband convinced her that it would make a gorgeous destination from their Paris mansion.

Years went into planning a paradise for their future children. At least quarterly each year, they visited the site from their base in France. Each time, Claire developed a stronger bond. Was it the land, the location, or the dream of a large white home with lacquered, dark green shuttered windows, and a giant, sparkling pool surrounded by flower and vegetable gardens which enticed her? Someday, two blonde and perfect children would ensure years of happiness in their euphoric paradise.
To the surprise of the couple, the land proved hardy and rich. Although surrounded by swamps, the land was black and appeared fertile. Christophe planted a trial garden. It consisted of tomatoes and brightly colored peppers. The fertility of the land surprised them. Not only did the seedlings grow rapidly, but they flourished. Locals commented that they had never witnessed such healthy and vibrant plants.

All of this persuaded the hesitant wife to build here, in this strange place. So, on a bright summer morning in June, the heavy equipment arrived with plans to build a ten-thousand square foot home of exquisite luxury. It would accompany a large pool as well as extensive flower and vegetable gardens. One side bordered a pristine lake of the bluest waters. Gentle winds seemed to blow consistently around this paradise.

The French couple's extended family was also excited. Everyone looked forward to spending glorious summers in the United States with this beloved duo. That was everyone except Aunt Michelle.

Uncle Louie's descendent, Michele, was ninety-seven years old. She was named for Louie's wife, Michelle Gautier, who lived during the earliest years of Louisiana history. During those early years, Louie's wife threatened to burn the Deed of Ownership to this awful land. The deed disappeared. The widow

Gautier thought that it was lost. That was good news! Michele knew the power of the innocent-looking place. Horrible repercussions existed whenever someone fell in love with *L'Euphorie.* The name was given many years earlier to this place of chaos, terror, and Cajun nightmares. Now, sadly Michelle flicked a tear from her wrinkled face.
"Please, not Claire and Christophe. What have they done?"
Christophe Gautier, born into a family of wealth and prestige in Paris, was showered with love from parents driven and stern. When he was born, they changed their earlier thoughts on rearing the only son born into the Gautier family in over twenty-five years. Instead of harshness, the couple doted. His every wish was their command.
A nanny gladly arrived at the elaborate home in Paris. Highly educated, she would tutor this exceptional child. Thrilled that they chose her over hundreds of applicants, she loved the

boy. As he grew, she became enthralled with him. Eventually, her motherly love changed into an intense desire for him. She lusted for the teenager. Soon, Madeline received payment from the boy's father, LaMar, to sleep with his only son. He was only fourteen years old.

Christophe believed this was normal. Always, he was given anything that he wanted. No person, place, or thing was off limits to him. Why had it taken so long for Madeline to give into his advances?

Such an event could have damaged the young boy, but it did not seem to cause serious repercussions. Christophe went to college with normal desires and expectations. He maintained a healthy love and admiration for women all of his life. Never did he harbor misogynist thoughts.

Not only did he possess unusual good looks, with his dark Cajun features, but academically he was at the top of his class. Obviously, he was gifted and talented. No woman was off limits to him. That is until he met Claire.

One summer day, just before summer vacation, the most beautiful woman walked past him on the college campus in Paris which they shared. Claire was tall and thin. Her long blond-white hair fell around her slim shoulders. Large eyes of the bluest azure looked at him. He melted. Never had desire overcome him to this extent. Claire appeared unnerved. Not remotely interested in him, she did not even smile as she strolled slowly past with her best friend, Adriana.

Claire desired to become a *pédiatre*. Nothing would stand in her way of becoming a doctor of children, she swore.

Christophe tried everything to gain her attention, but it was all in vain. Eventually, he called on his father, LaMar, to help. Claire's family was prosperous but not in the Gautier family's league. LaMar called her *Père*. The two fathers scheduled lunch at Gautier's club for the young people. Soon afterward, Claire agreed to attend a party with the handsome son. The rest was history.

Their attraction was strong. Immediately after graduation, they married. Young Claire never realized that such a life waited for her. Each day, flowers filled the ten room apartment which she and Christophe shared in Paris.

Papa Gautier welcomed the couple back from Belize, where they celebrated a month-long honeymoon, to a grand 6,500 square foot home. Nestled in the 18th Arrondissement, they enjoyed a view of the Eiffel Tower each day from the balcony which surrounded them. French-white walls reflected the softest hint of blue. Eighteen-foot ceilings soared with a faint cobalt glow. Although the structure dated back to 1929, recent renovations tastefully demonstrated the latest in technology as well as gorgeous accessories.

The first day back, Claire could hardly wait for her new husband to leave for the office he shared with his father. Like a young child, she ran from room to room touching and spinning until she was dizzy. The excitement pulsed through her young body making it impossible to contain.

"Mama, you must come to our home. It is *magnifique!*"

Of course, Mama came at once. The two women were inseparable. Daily exercise at the Ritz-Carlton followed by two-hour lunches was the rule, not the exception. Claire also surrounded herself with young women who were captivated not just by her intellect but her vast wealth.

Dreams of a selfless life of medicine quickly were forgotten. Life was too much fun to add misery and misfortune to the equation. She dreamed of a little white-haired boy and girl with azure eyes.

Christophe thrived under his Papa's tutelage. The making of money came effortlessly for him as it had for his ancestors. He adored his new wife and home. Life could not be more idyllic. Years trickled past. Only happiness graced the young family. Their joy shrouded them in love. The land waited silently for the arrival of the future owners of the most beautiful antebellum home in the New Orleans area. Deep in the transition zone of the earth, something trembled.

## TWO: THE LOUISIANA PURCHASE

Several members of the Gautier family migrated from France to the United States in the mid-seventeen hundreds. They settled in the area of Louisiana. This group of French settlers continued to use their language as well as their previous Catholic religion. Uncle Louie's relatives were a part of this migration of people who were called *Cajun.* One such relative was Louie's grandfather, Leo.

Louie eventually inherited the Midas Touch from Leo. Every business deal which Leo conducted became gold. He purchased large plots of land in Louisiana, just before the authority to the Louisiana Territory was transferred. Thomas Jefferson may have negotiated *The Deal of the Century*, but the Gautier family conducted plenty of impressive transactions.

Before his death, Leo divided these large plots. He created various subdivisions.

All of this eventually was bestowed to Leo's son, Boyce who eventually left the land to his only son, Louie.

Louie loved to visit his vast estate. Regularly, he enjoyed riding his horse into the brush while there. When conditions overpowered him, the young man dismantled and walked. On a sunny autumn day, as he walked among the dense brush, he discovered an incredible site. As he pushed the branches apart, to his amazement, there existed a large piece of land covered in the greenest of grass. Large oaks and magnolias towered as low-growing flowering shrubs such as pink azalea beckoned entry to this magical piece of ground. The young Frenchman discovered a small lake of pure, clear cobalt blue water. Resting under the biggest oak tree, near the border of the water, he fell asleep.

Dreams of his past cascaded before him. He remembered things which he had forgotten years ago. When he awoke, he sat up with a smile. Where had all of those thoughts originated? Suddenly, he felt rejuvenated and free from the aches which his joints had developed. He rushed away. Still, the next day, his thoughts were drawn back to that mysterious place.

Day after day, he returned to sleep under the old tree by the perfect, little lake. This strange tree appeared ancient. His dreams continued to inspire him with good thoughts. Until, a blustery, wintry wind blew from the north-side of the property. Tossing and turning, dreams became nightmares. He felt as though he was his father. Suddenly, dreams were of Boyce, not himself. If his father had done these horrible things, which Louie dreamed, he was not the man that his son once believed.

Tormented, by these continual, obsessive thoughts, he returned to the sick bed of his beloved father in France. Kneeling by his side, he repeated the visions which refused to leave. Sadly,

Boyce, his Père, admitted that at one time, he killed several men over a land dispute. It was brutal. Louie's tears fell onto the ill man's lips. Softly, the father begged forgiveness. Louie confirmed that he understood that Boyce did these things for the family. In his heart, those previous actions broke the love he harbored. Boyce was no longer the perfect hero to his son. Although all of the wealth and lands which belonged to Leo would now pass from Boyce to Louie, he felt betrayed by the actions of his father. Was he a hypocrite for loving the land purchased by spilled blood? Once he returned to Louisiana, Louie could not refrain from the majestic, green pastures which he owned. Even in the rain and cold, he slept under the old tree. Visions of generational sins paraded before his eyes. Some days, the dreams were only of his life. Other days, they were of unknown relatives. Once, he witnessed the rape of his wife at the hands of an old friend. He knew that it was true. During that time, Michelle appeared withdrawn and unhappy. She refused to discuss the reason. He had suspected an affair between his beloved wife and the local landowner, Hugo Dubois. Never would Michelle admit to it.

Anger burned in Louie's soul at the transgression committed by Hugo. They once were college roommates. How could this have happened? When he confronted his old friend in a local Louisiana pub, Hugo laughed and responded with taunts.

"Michelle deserved what happened. She pranced around in front of your pals. Don't you know that she was a tease? I did you a favor."

Louie only knew that no one deserved the actions forced on the woman whom he loved. He challenged his friend to a duel. Following proper protocol, he shot his friend in the heart. No charges were filed against Louie. Those were the ways back then. Another murder occurred over a land dispute involving the enchanting plot of earth in Louisiana. Michelle always blamed herself for Hugo's death and the loss of respect from her husband. Michelle had done nothing to cause the rape. Still, the relationship between the husband and wife deteriorated. Just as love succumbed from the heart of Louie for his father, Boyce. No love remained in the once happy home shared by Louie and his beloved wife. Louie found a mistress while Michelle found solace in her lovely flower garden of red and pink roses.

In her heart, Michelle remembered her husband's tales of enchantment on the beautiful plot of land located deep in a bayou of Louisiana. His frequent visits there seemed to change him. Occasionally, he mentioned *generational sins.*

More and more, Louie remained in Louisiana instead of Paris. Michelle tried to find the land deed. For the well-being of her family, she must destroy it. Louie insisted that he lost the land in a poker match. Michelle had smiled with relief. That was all a lie. Generations later, a beloved nephew was determined to build a home for his future children in a place that Michelle had hated. A place which destroyed her marriage, where many men died. What would it destroy for the handsome Christophe and Claire?

# THREE: THE MAISON BEGINS

On a sunny June morning, the front-end loaders and workmen arrived at the magical land outside of New Orleans. It was an exciting time. Mosquitoes hung in the dense forage. Humid, languid days baked in the hot, Louisiana sun. Nothing mattered to Christophe. His mind paraded the future home past his eyes. He could feel the happiness waiting for Claire and himself. An inherent love burned in this young man's breast for the land which many had died to protect.

His beloved wife was always beside him during the building process. Smothered with suntan lotion and mosquito repellent, she smiled from her large, straw hat at the antics of Christophe. Each detail of *La Maison Blanche* was perfected. It would be a site to behold. Gorgeous landscaping added the final touch to the house with southern charm. The white house with dark green shutters appeared to step out of pages from the past. It was an antebellum plantation that Louie would have loved. Oak trees and pink azaleas marked the inner boundaries of the magnificent property. A pristine lake of blue waters gently ushered north winds into the branches of trees and a variety of flowering shrubs.

Exactly two years after the groundbreaking, four large moving trucks arrived filled with breathtaking indoor and outdoor furniture to the sparkling *White House.*

Neighbors traveled many miles to witness a vast display of wealth transferred to their area. Such a stylish home provided many jobs for the community. Exactly nine months later, a baby girl was born.

The *White House* proudly welcomed the first Christophe Gautier child to its fold. Little Claire, named for generations of Bernard daughters, followed as a carbon copy of her beautiful mother.

Christophe carried the baby over the threshold as his wife happily watched from the sweeping veranda on their return from the local hospital. Now, their home was complete. If only a little boy might follow someday.

Joyfully, *bébé* Claire spent her days at the *White House*. Happiness filled the passages of this grand palace. Laughter bounced off the walls. Claire renamed the house *Joyeux*.

Bébé Claire's first word was "joyeux." Her parents thought it strange but laughed as they hugged her softly.

Years progressed, the baby Claire grew taller and stronger. The child was home-educated by a French nanny in the confines of *Joyeux* which pleased her. The family found it difficult to leave this place of enchantment. They extended no invitations for visits to their French family which seemed odd. Nothing mattered to the handsome couple but the idyllic life which waited each day behind these private, shiny white walls.

Long, lazy days were spent in the infinity pool as the couple watched young Claire swim. She was like a tadpole in the water. No water wings or life vests were needed. Her skill in the water was impressive.

After a year, Claire and her husband finally left the home for an overnight trip to New Orleans. They had not returned to the Paris mansion in over three years. It was time for a break from the perfect life. Excitedly, they visited the French Quarter and Garden District of New Orleans inside this spin-off of French delights. Their time there was treasured. When they returned home, many presents accompanied them.

The nanny, Alice, met them at the door. *"M. Christophe, Le Bébé se promène!"* Although this announcement was not unusual, most babies walk between nine and twelve months, to Claire and Christophe, it was heart-breaking. They missed seeing her first little steps.

Claire ran up the stairs to the pink and white nursery. Slowly, she opened the door. The young child was hugging the wall. Quietly, she mumbled something which was incoherent. Claire watched in fascination as the baby kissed the wall and gently stroked the glistening white surface. The young mother swore that she felt the house shake.

Christophe laughed at the absurdity of her remarks.

"Claire, this is ridiculous! Are you saying that our precious child caused the house to tremble? That is a little silly, don't you think?"

His wife refused to change her account. Who knows when they may have returned to France? Eventually, a business problem forced Chris to go back. Reluctantly, the entire family, including Nanny, flew back to a home which they once adored in the bustling city of Paris.

 While in *The City of Lights* many overlooked issues needed to be addressed. Time flew. Claire discovered that she carried a baby boy. Their joy was uncontrollable. They settled all problems quickly so that they could rush back to *Joyful* with excitement.

A new nursery needed completion. Seven months later, a baby boy joined the Gautier family. Christophe chose the name Coty. There had been several men and women named such in past generations of his family. The name in French means *living by a river bank.* This title seemed appropriate because a small lake splashed gently on the northside of the property. Just like his sister, the young lad loved to swim. He always chose the clear waters of his beloved lake. Christophe spent long days with his son tubing and relaxing by the river edge as Claire and bébé Claire puttered by the pool. Eventually, the baby girl was just called "Babe." It was easier to differentiate between the two females. Life was good.

## FOUR: STRANGE OCCURRENCES

As the years continued past, on this family who lived in *Joyful*, the young mother noticed unusual things about the relationship between her young children and the *White House*. Often, she entered a room to find Babe and Coty standing together facing a wall in the nursery. They talked in their limited vocabulary as though the walls were real.
There was difficulty whenever the couple tried to leave the walls of their home. The children would cry and reach out to the house. Their papa assumed that the beauty of the place was the draw. Not many other spaces offered such beautiful accommodations.
Both toddlers loved their nurseries. Frequently, they hugged the walls or kissed them. Such behavior began to appear normal. When Claire entered Babe's room to discover Alice, the nanny, kissing the wall that was a little too much.

"Alice, why would you kiss the walls?" She was shocked.

The young nanny explained that she witnessed the children do this so often that she had begun to do the same. Soon, Claire found that she enjoyed touching the walls. Once, she kissed the sparkling, satiny white wall, for the house was painted various shades of white inside and out. Just one kiss led to a fascination. Quickly, she not only lovingly stroked the paneled surface, but she also talked to the house with deep love. It was as though the house nodded in agreement. Christophe was unaware of the strange attraction between his family and their home.

A cloudy, chilly January day brought plans for a large birthday party to celebrate Babe's fifth birthday. Such an event brought locals scurrying to the Gautier home for a party unlike anything that they ever witnessed. Ponies walked freely around the green grass as well as a band playing Babe's favorite songs.

Festivities showered down. Rain soon showered as well. This change in the weather forced the party indoors. No matter, there was plenty of room. Five year old Babe led the procession of children up to her nursery.

"I am going to insist that Mama redoes my room. This place looks like a baby's room."

She announced to her friends. The others only wished that they possessed such a beautiful space.

All of the boys accompanied Coty to his room where he told how much he loved his home. Soon, a fight ensued between Coty and his best friend, Arthur. That little boy thought that Babe was the most beautiful girl in the world. Young Arthur also thought that the Gautier family were braggarts. At least, that's what his father often said about them. Arthur said things which a small boy should not repeat.

Coty didn't understand but knew that such things were not nice. He demanded that Arthur leave. All of the children followed them to the top of the stairs. Arthur became defiant as he insulted the entire Gautier family, even Coty's mom, Claire. The disagreement intensified as Coty stood his ground against the boy. Arthur considered pushing his best friend Coty down the stairs; never had the two boys been so upset. The others laughed at them. At that moment, the house seemed to shake. To Coty's amazement, Arthur fell down the steep stairs. As his body bounced and splattered out of control, the children stood in silence at the top of the staircase. When the small form rested at the bottom, the children began to scream in hysteria at the profuse blood covering the scene. All of the parents ran to the horrible accident. Arthur's mother, Rebecca, grabbed the broken, bloodied body of her child. Silently, she clutched him to her heart. No one spoke for the longest time.

The children confirmed that Arthur seemed to miss a step and plummeted down to his death. Coty cried for days at the terrible thing which happened to his friend. He never described the desire which overcame him to push his friend or the feeling that the house moved. The young boy suffered in silence for the loss of his best friend without understanding what happened. He never blamed himself, but he always remembered the flash before his eyes as though he witnessed the event before it occurred when he felt the house shake.

## FIVE: YEARS PASS

Thirteen years flew past at the beautiful *Joyful.* The entire family grew closer to each other and the lovely home. The bond between the house and Claire solidified. It became harder and harder for her to leave her splendid mansion. On a lovely, sapphire summer day, Babe announced that she wanted to return to Paris for her *universite´* days. Claire and Christophe were surprised. Coty then stated that he wanted to go back to France for his studies in two years. Babe also informed her family that she had gained acceptance at the Pierre and Marie Curie University, which was rated ninth on the list of the best global universities in the world and first on the list of the best global universities in France. No one was aware that young Claire had even applied.

The lovely campus sat close to *La Seine on the Quai Saint Bernard.* The location in the Latin Quarter of the 5th arrondissement of Paris pleased Babe's mom. Secretly, Claire missed the excitement of Paris. Babe's choice demanded that the family leave their beautiful home in the states and travel once again.

The lovely home shook at this announcement. How could her beloved family, which she had sheltered and protected, even consider leaving her? It was as though something came alive in the house. A strong emotion shook the very foundation of the sparkling structure. Anger trembled in the peaceful building which was an emotion never before experienced.

Babe looked at the family as they felt the quiver from deep in the bowels of the massive structure. She realized that this news upset her beloved house. A little fear spread silently in her heart. How could she explain that a power stronger than her love for the beautiful *Joyeux* drove her? She loved her birth country just as much as her adopted one.

Many family members and friends remained in Paris. Years may have passed, but her relationship remained devoted to those dear people. They would all finally be united for the adventure of their lives as she and her brother Coty studied for careers in research in the *City of Lights*. The house felt betrayed by all of this.

*Joyeux* tried to understand the apparent anticipation and excitement of the family. She could not. The only thing that felt sure was a betrayal. Yes, she continued to protect and shelter these four people, but sadness now flowed through the walls.

Claire felt the change. So did Babe. They passed in the halls and lovingly stroked the walls. **House** must understand how much this meant to the women of the family. At least that's what they told each other.

# SIX: ANOTHER STRANGE DEATH

The women of the Gautier family shopped all summer for their return to Paris and university days for the children. Even though he was too young to begin studies, Coty requested to stay with family members until his time arrived for study. Confident that he would gain acceptance, he dreamed of studying soon to enter research at the same university as his sister. What a pair these talented youth would become. Although they were sad at the empty nest which would result, Christophe and Claire looked forward to all of the dreams which they could now fulfill. Claire dreamed of long, lazy days puttering in her gardens while Christophe wrote his fantasy novel. What a way to finish their lives not only fulfilling their destiny, but enjoying their private heaven.

The day of departure for Paris finally arrived. All of the bags were loaded by

Charles, the butler, into the family Range Rover. Their private jet stood fueled and ready for take-off. The weather was perfect for the long flight. Babe walked the halls of her beloved *Joyeux* with tears streaming from her blue eyes. Lovingly, she stroked the walls, but something was very wrong. No love flowed back to her from the satiny, white paneling. What was wrong? This loss of connection caused her more pain at leaving. The young woman loved **House**; it wasn't that her feelings had changed, but she felt her destiny waited in France.

Her mother discovered Babe kneeling on the floor as she implored **House** to understand why she must leave. "Mama, she does not understand. **House** now hates me. There is no love here." Claire pulled the distraught girl up into her arms. As she embraced the tearful young woman, she pulled disheveled hair from her young eyes.

"She must understand. I will deal with her when I return. You must be joyful at your decision. Do not let her pull you back. Go forward with your plans. Perhaps, Papa and I will bring a few orphans to reside here. **House** will understand. She fears emptiness, but we will not let that occur. Now, it is time to leave. Nanny will stay here while we are gone. I told her to sleep late for a change. Let's depart!"

Joy did spring back from the saddened blue eyes of the young woman. Quickly, Babe stroked the wall of **House**, kissed it, as she sweetly called, *"Au revoir, Ma Maison, bien-aimée!"*

**House** shook after they left. With so much intensity, it trembled and awoke Nanny in the downstairs, corner bedroom. For the first time, since arriving here, Alice felt fear. Doing just as she witnessed Claire and Babe do, she ran to the wall of her room and stroked it. Soothingly, she mumbled in her lovely, French voice to the angry **House**.

Reports stated that the jet crashed as it ascended on take-off. Everyone died instantly.

Nanny was cutting roses in the garden when the authorities arrived with news. Screams of horror resonated within the walls of **House** all during the night. The young woman could not believe that her family had died. She felt that somehow, **House** was involved in the demise of her employers. Rage enveloped her. Her fists of hatred pummeled the walls which once knew only strokes of love and respect. Nanny screamed disgust and betrayal at this place of control. Mistakenly, she blamed **House** for the death of her beloved family. **House** did not understand what had occurred. Why was the family not coming back? The crash was mechanical. Alice never received the actual report.

"I will leave at once, as soon as light appears. A taxi will arrive for me. Never, will I return to you. You are not good. You are chaos and tragedy! How dare you? I know what you are. The world will know."

**House** rumbled deeply from within the foundations. Did this woman think that she could hurt something with ties to the very earth on which she stood? Well, she would see about that. How dare this Nanny think that **House** would hurt someone that she adored. Yes, she may have caused Arthur's demise, but he threatened Coty. However, she would never hurt one whom she loved.

Faithful to her words, Nanny rose from her bed. She packed her bags and carried them to the front door. Not even waiting for help with them, the grieving young woman lined them in a row by the front entrance. Sadly, she drank coffee alone in the great kitchen which had sheltered only happy get-togethers in the past. The taxi arrived right on time. The young driver whistled as he beheld the sight of such wealth. Admiringly, he rubbed the white boards of the palatial structure. He rang the chimes. Nanny ran toward the stairs. She held onto the railing as she began to descend. Just as she raised her right foot, the house shook strongly. A large crystal chandelier gracefully provided light for the dark stairs. Quickly, it fell. Such a massive fixture crushed the petite frame of Alice. Her head bent in an impossible way. Her neck snapped as her pulverized body rested under the intense weight. **House** smiled, "Well, Alice won't be leaving me, at least, not alive."

No matter to **House**, nothing mattered anymore. No one would ever be welcomed here again. This home, after all, was *Claire's House.* **House** never understood the loss of the beloved ones. How could anyone ever blame her for the demise of the Gautier family? She was indeed innocent of that one!

# SEVEN: NEXT VICTIM!

Steven and Lorraine Hinckley descended from generations who had resided in the New Orleans area since the Louisiana Purchase. The Cajun blood ran deep as did love for this strange and bold area. Being empty-nesters now for many years had caused a stirring deep within their hearts for a connection with their family. Children and grandchildren created a large clan for them. They tired of the Garden District within the city. Daily traffic problems and growing numbers of people created tension in their lives. For many years, the two discussed moving out from the hectic life that now surrounded them. Their children had moved away long ago. Now, they visited for weeks at a time to enjoy not only their parents, but the little slice of heaven within the gates of their estate. What they all needed was a larger slice of paradise where they could gather under one roof and spend longer hours together.

One day, Lorraine saw an advertisement within the glossy pages of her favorite magazine. *Joyeux* seemed to call to her from the boundary of page seventy-one. Over drinks that evening, she showed the picture of the mansion to Steven. He groaned. Never did he think that she would consider leaving the city which they had loved for so long. Surely, she wasn't serious? Reluctantly, he agreed to accompany Lorraine and her best friend Jenny, the real estate agent, for a look. That was all it would be, just a quick look.

On a sunny, cloudless, Louisiana-blue sky day, the three meandered through the locked gates of the beautiful *Joyeux*. From the moment they entered the confines of her borders, they were all hypnotized by the graceful southern charm of the plantation. The two women grabbed each other frequently as they pointed at indescribable beauty. Such elegant detailing was indeed rare even at this price. Steven admitted that he felt something visceral about the place. They studied each inch of the grand house with deep fascination. The extensive gardens they saved for a later day. Hours slowly ticked on the massive clock in the hall. **House** smiled. Lorraine could imagine all of the children and grandkids under one roof for extended summer visits. There would certainly be plenty of room here. Even though their current home was large inside New Orleans, it was impossible for them to all stay at one time. A few always retreated to a hotel, so they were scattered. The family had never enjoyed a time where they all remained together the entire time. Lorraine laughed with glee as she considered that Ben would no longer be able to bring his mistress to the hotel that he and her daughter Lory shared with their children. What revenge!

Steven thought about his slutty daughter-in-law and the disagreements he had heard through closed doors when they gathered with the family. His son, Clint, hated the way she flirted at the bar where they were forced to stay. Now, no more bars for Jennifer to flaunt her beauty. Yes, things just got challenging for the Hinckley family.

Lorraine turned to her husband late that afternoon with a large smile.

"What do you think? Finally, our family can all be together. Don't you know that the children will love it at that big ole house and the fact that we will all be under one roof at last? Many wrongs, we can finally settle in our family." Devilish grins spread across their faces as they considered the pain this situation would cause their spoiled and whiny kids. The couple loved their children but being with them for long periods of time was extremely difficult even if they did stay in a hotel much of the time. They had reared a spoiled and privileged group of whiners! Maybe, they would hate to be crowded together under the watchful eye of "mom and dad." The parents didn't care about their selfish wants. The only thing important to them was their grandchildren.

The next day, Steven returned with a few of his buddies to walk some of the twenty acres of his next possible home. The remainder of the land was too swampy to create interest. His friends loved it as much as he. Geoffrey told him that if he didn't purchase it, he would. This statement put a little pressure on Mr. Hinckley to make a quicker choice. He rushed home that night with the proclamation that they, "Must buy *Joyeux* immediately."

Lorraine smiled. Jenny's husband and a few of her friends had done an excellent job of convincing Steven. The large commission could more than cover Jenny's promise of a small percentage to each of the men who participated in convincing Mr. Hinckley of the wisdom of purchasing the house. What were friends for if not to lead each other through such difficult decisions? The real estate agent phoned the two men excitedly.

"Good job, they should ask me to write a contract tomorrow. I bet they close quickly! We will enjoy lots of great parties with the Hinckley couple very soon. They have become so boring lately compared to all of the expensive parties that they once threw. Maybe this new property will put some life back in our social scene. Not to mention all of the money that I will make." She laughed with glee as she promised each of them a split.

Just as she predicted, the next morning, her phone rang at the ungodly hour of 8 am. A smile greeted her lips as she heard the gushy voice of Lorraine asking to meet at the club for lunch. All was progressing as planned; everyone in her office would be so jealous of this huge commission! Now, her husband Bart would take her on that river cruise to Paris.

One month later, Steven drove his wife through the gates and refurbished property of *Joyeux*.

"How did you do all of this? You kept telling me that you just couldn't get workers to complete it. Steven, it is breath-taking. I can't wait for the children to see it!"

He loved to spoil his wife. Lorraine was his joy. The house may indeed be "joyous," but his wife imparted genuine happiness to him. For hours, they walked together through the many rooms of their new home. Nothing had gone beyond his scrutiny except for a paver on the outside patio. It had never set correctly among the other bricks. Instead, the left corner jutted out sharply. Oh well, just a little glitch. Nothing over which to be concerned. They would repair that later.

Inside **House,** everything remained just as Claire and Christophe left it when they took Babe and Coty back to Paris on that fateful flight. Family members had removed their clothes and a few paintings. Everything else looked as if **House** waited in anticipation of the Gautier family's return. A detailed power wash did wonders for the exterior.

Lorraine distributed furniture from the city home among the five children. Their home inside of New Orleans sold quickly. Jenny retired from the real estate business which she hated. Now, she and her husband had enough extra cash to travel as they had dreamed. Everyone had won on this transaction. Everyone did seem to win except **House.** She frowned at the matronly Lorraine with her squeaky voice. The demands which she seemed to place on everyone around her were irritating. Never would **House** recover from the loss of her beautiful mistress. This residence, after all, was *Claire's House.* No other mistress would ever compare.

**House** immediately decided that she would not protect these overweight, chirpy people. They needed to go.
The Hinckley couple planned a lavish summer party. All of the children and grandchildren arrived. Things were happy for only a few hours. Ben, their son-in-law, kept leaving to check on his mistress. His action created tears for Lory, the Hinckley daughter. Everyone knew where he was going and what he was doing. The children knew as well. They weren't idiots.
Jennifer complained to Clint that they should take their kids to the Hotel Roosevelt. All of the family under one roof was a little too much closeness for her. Clint smiled with delight. *Mother sure knows how to control our family.* Finally, he could sleep without worrying about what his wife was up to at the bar. The remainder of the five children and grandkids got on well together. They loved the place. They played in the pool most of the day. Steven suggested that

they cancel the club membership because the house provided all that they needed. The drive was too long now. After a few drinks, someone may be hurt. Everyone laughed. Life was good. Later in the evening, many drinks were consumed with a delicious dinner compliments of their private chef. Maybe having all of them under one roof wasn't such a good idea because everyone drank way too much.
Tempers flared even among the thoughtful children. Those without mistresses and slutty wives became emotional with each other. Angry words hurled into the hot, humid night.
Clint pushed Jennifer into the pool. Ben left to be with his mistress over pleas that he remain. It was a nightmare. Betsy and her husband had a major fight. He rushed back to the city. A call came late in the evening that her husband, Stewart, was arrested for a DUI. The other daughter and her husband weren't talking while Amy and

Matt, the youngest of the Hinckley family, held hands long into the darkness. They had not noticed all the drama.

Slowly, the next morning, the children left the grand gates of *Joyeux*. **House** smiled. Only Amy and Matt remained. Lorraine cried all day. Steven left to bail Stewart from jail. What had they done? Months passed. Lorraine and Steven dreaded the thought of gathering the family for a repeat. At least, Ben and Lory were divorced. He could now live with his mistress, and Lory may find someone else. Then, maybe their daughter's life would not be unbearable. No one had ever liked Ben; they were better off without him.

Slowly, the summer waned. Soon, a New Year came without fanfare at *La Maison Blanche.* Lorraine and Steven wowed their friends with a massive party. Everyone loved the grand mansion even though it remained empty except for Lorraine and Steven.

**House** tolerated her matronly new charge. Lorraine's voice grated on the structure, but **House** tried to accept the change. Dreams of the beautiful two women who once resided here kept **House** in-check. No one could ever replace those two!

As the years passed, Lorraine and Steven enjoyed their life together. The children and grandchildren never came again. That was just as well. Life became peaceful. Days flowed into each other without drama.

Suddenly, one early November day, Lorraine burst into Steven's study. Her peaceful demeanor had changed to one of passion and excitement.

"We simply must plan a large gathering for this Christmas. What is our problem? Years are flying past. We have lost valuable time with the family. Let's plan something incredible. We'll have a famous band and fireworks. Our family will love it!"

**House** groaned. *Not those spoiled brats again. I thought that they were gone forever.*

Then **House** smiled. She had not wanted to cause a disaster. The Hinckley crew weren't bad people, just irritating. Still, they needed to go.

Lorraine called a friend, Jill, the event planner. Yes, she would take over all the plans. Lorraine only needed to relax and enjoy the show. **House** smiled. Yes, this would be a show.

Weeks of preparation and plans slowly evolved into the event of a lifetime. Reluctantly, the children assembled again for a week of family misery. Lory brought her new love, Ted. The family must welcome him.

On December 23, they all arrived. Each played their role. The family hierarchy sprang into play. That day and night passed without problems. Everyone behaved.

Finally, Christmas Day arrived. Tons of presents waited under the massive tree.

Wrapping paper, strewn from one end of the sunny white-yellow room to the other, caused smiles from the parents. It was a good thing that Lorraine hired extra help.

Finally, the big night arrived. The band played music from the sixties. Friends of the children and grandchildren danced gaily. Lots of booze flowed. The Hinckley family glowed with excitement and pride.

Late in the night, festivities continued. The meal was over. Chef had outdone himself with delicious Chateaubriand for all. The mood was happy. Steven smiled as he watched his love, Lorraine, enjoy her fifth martini. It had been a long night, but no one wanted it to end.

They all moved to the pool. This day, the weather had been exceptionally sunny and warm for a winter's day. Some of the kids entered the pool dressed in their finest. It didn't matter. They didn't worry over trivia such as replacing outlandishly priced attire.

# CLAIRE'S HOUSE

Lorraine heard the splashes outside as she wearily climbed the inside stairs destined for her bed. She couldn't remember ever drinking so much. Suddenly, something shook deep within her. She and Steven must make this home fun if they were to enjoy years of family bliss. Running down the stairs, she bolted out the door to the pool. Everyone pointed and laughed at her exuberance. Then, she fell. Her foot caught in the paver which jutted out. The fall was hard. Her face plowed into the stone. Her cranium split open from the impact. Blood gushed from the broken site on her head. Steven collapsed. **House** smiled.

"Another one is gone. Now, maybe Claire will return?" **House** just could not understand where her beautiful French family had gone.

## EIGHT: A NEW PERSON

Steven mourned for his beloved Lorraine. After her burial, he stopped his biweekly golf game and lunch at the club. More and more, the lonely widower withdrew to the walls of the *White House.*
There, alone, he found solace. Lorraine's staff cared for him as though he was their family. The maid, Roberta, moved closer to his room. It seemed that the more he removed himself from the public, the more he desired aloneness within the beautiful walls of **House.** Each day, he enjoyed the pool and sunning on the banks of his alluring lake. Although he missed Lorraine, he wasn't lonely. Instead, he developed a bond with **House**. Steven remained of sound mind. It wasn't that he snapped; the solitude of **House** comforted his weary spirit. Outside, life no longer appeared attractive. Everyone seemed boring or taxing on his nerves. Only

**House** understood the sadness which draped over the broken man.
One day, as he sunbathed by the lake, a gorgeous young woman walked slowly toward him.
"Hello, Steven, do you remember me?" Tall, blonde, with legs that appeared longer than her body, she strolled closer.
"Claire?" He remembered the previous owner of the *White House*. Her beauty was legendary in the area. Of course, Steven knew that she died in a plane crash. How did she get here? Briefly, he considered that he may have lost his mind.
"Steven, it isn't Claire. Thank you for the compliment. She was the most gorgeous woman that I ever saw."
The young beauty smiled briefly. He melted into the chaise lounge.
"Steven, it is Clarissa Grant. Don't you remember me? I'm the daughter of Jim and Gloria Grant. You and my father were friends long before Lorraine's

death. Don't you remember all of the events at the club?"

Clarissa's dad passed away years ago. There were rumors in town that Jim had lost his mind. Clarissa's mother suffered from Alzheimers Disease since the death of her beloved husband. The young woman was the same age as Steven's daughter, Lory.

Hours passed as the two sat by the rippling waters of the deep, blue waters of the lake. The perfect day floated away slowly before their eyes. It amazed Steven that with the age difference so many memories and enjoyments were being shared. Clarissa seemed more like a close friend to him than a friend to his daughter.

Steven invited Clarissa to join him for dinner later that evening.

**House** quivered as the woman walked into her arms. For a brief moment, she thought that it was Claire. **House** loved beauty. Dowdy, overweight Lorraine depressed **House.** This woman portrayed style and elegance. For the first time, since the death of Babe and Claire, **House** radiated happiness and joy.

Steven commented, "The house has come alive again since your arrival, Clarissa."

He did not want the young beauty to leave his side. She may come to her senses and not desire his company. Before she left, on that special night, she kissed him gently on the lips. Steven wondered, that kiss, was it the kiss of a daughter or lover? **House** knew and finally felt happy again. She always got just what she wanted one way or another.

## NINE: LOVE BLOOMS

**House** smiled on the beautiful Clarissa. Her elegance and style reflected the very beauty which Claire and Christophe lovingly envisioned here so long ago. Each day, Clarissa came to nurse Steven's broken spirit. As he healed and his grief subsided, he became aware how damaged he was since the death of his beloved Lorraine. Now, he thrilled to the new, fresh love of a beautiful, younger woman.
On a cloudy, rainy night, Steven requested that Cook plan Clarissa's favorite meal. Clarissa felt deep in her spirit that something special was about to occur. She wore a red, sheer dress. Red was Steven's favorite color. Lorraine hated red. She didn't get it. Lorraine thought of it as tawdry. Secretly, Steven never told her how much he loved the thrill of a beautiful red color.

The table glowed in the candlelight of long, tapered, white candles. A gleaming, crystal bowl graced the center of the table with dark red roses. It was obviously not a typical night.
Excitement bounced from the white walls of **House**.
The couple enjoyed a toast to each other, "A long and happy future" was lovingly proposed by Steven. Clarissa's blue eyes shined with love.
Steven suddenly walked to her. He took her left hand and kneeled by her side. Out of his jacket, he produced a dark gray, velvet box. A gold ring held a huge diamond which reflected multiple colors within the shine which it produced. Lovingly, he asked Clarissa to marry him. As close as they had become, she was not aware that he returned her love. Never, did she dream that he would invite her into his world. Tearily, she expressed doubts about how his children may receive her. Steven assured her that they would lovingly welcome her. In

their hearts, they both wanted deeply to believe this, but it did not seem likely. Lory, Steven's daughter, had been a good friend many years ago to Clarissa. She had always appeared spoiled and selfish. Clarissa doubted that a second wife would be wanted by the Hinckley clan. Especially one that was her age. Still, she accepted his proposal while hoping that she was doing the right thing for Steven.

A few weeks passed. Their contentment grew. They decided to invite all the family for a long weekend. None of the children had been back to the *White House* since Lorraine's death. They all hated the place which they dubbed the *White Elephant*. **House** didn't care. She hated everyone except Steven and now, Clarissa.

The group arrived. It was a late fall evening. The wind gently blew. Everyone waited by the pool for Cook to announce "dinner is served."

No one could figure out what was wrong with Steven. He appeared nervous. As they enjoyed drinks, the butler whispered something to Steven. He held up his hand and exited the scene. Probably some business call, they thought.

Everyone watched in amazement as he returned with one of their friends. The kids rushed to Clarissa's side. She was a debutante and hugely popular in New Orleans. They assumed that her invitation was for their enjoyment. The small group of young adults gathered around in fascination. Her beauty was soft, southern, almost fragile.

When Steven took her hand, the kids thought it was a joke. Everyone laughed gaily. Then, the couple took each other's hands. The ring glowed in the semi-darkness. Lovingly, with soft voices, they described what happened within the walls of **House**. The family wanted to be angry. How dare this young woman steal the place of saintly Lorraine? It was impossible to express anger inside of **House**. Instead, gushing words of happiness and kisses swallowed the beautiful Clarissa. The Hinckley children felt that they lost control of their ability to express themselves. Words of kindness and acceptance were not what they intended. They looked at each other confused over their words of gushiness. Clarissa could not believe how quickly they accepted her. The couple felt, in their hearts, that they would encounter violent protests and anger. The approval of the Hinckley children was easier than anyone could dream. **House** quivered. Things were perfect at last. All of her plans clicked. The children's words were not what they wanted to say. Those were the words of **House.**

## Ten: The Wedding

**House** had never looked this elegant. Wine-colored roses mixed with white long-stemmed ones cascaded down the railings of the grand staircase. That June day, when Clarissa became Mrs. Steven Hinckley, glowed without a cloud. Clarissa wanted an indoor wedding. Steven would have given his new wife anything. Never, would he forget the way that she looked as she walked down the stairs in a Vera Wang wedding gown. The Mulberry silk cream dress fit the thin frame of Clarissa like a glove. Tiny pearls edged the bodice and skirt. Long sleeves adorned her graceful hands. She was exquisite. The bride carried a bouquet of red and white roses with baby's breath intermingled. Champagne flowed like water. The finest caterers in New Orleans proudly displayed their imaginative dishes. The local press covered each and every detail.

The couple invited their friends as did the children and grandchildren. A total of eight hundred people proudly walked the grounds dressed for a ball. The wedding was a white tie event. The friends, fortunate enough to be invited, would never forget the evening. Exactly at 7 pm, the harp softly strummed with a full-string orchestra Wagner's *Bridal Chorus*. Everyone stood and turned to witness an angel floating down the stairs on the arm of her brother. **House** beamed with pride. This home may be *Claire's House*, but Clarissa experienced the same degree of love and respect from this antebellum masterpiece. This house belonged to Claire. **House** missed her. Not only her exquisite beauty but the gay laughter which echoed down the halls. When Babe entered the family, the euphoria of **House** could never again be repeated. Still, Clarissa was a softer version of the original owner. **House** caressed her and Steven in protection.

The exuberance of the guests as Mr. and Mrs. Hinckley exited to the beloved *Somewhere Over the Rainbow* brought tears to the eyes of men and women. **House** shook slightly with emotion. The mood remained festive but respectful the entire evening. Guests could not pry their eyes off the stunning couple. Clarissa danced with her husband all through the night. The bride did not want a honeymoon. Her desire was to remain by the banks of their beloved lake at *La Maison Blanche*. Steven hung a small wooden sign by the shore of the blue water proclaiming *Clarissa's Lake*. The sign by the front gate remained *This is Claire's House*. Clarissa felt it would be disrespectful to remove the reminder of the one who built this place of beauty.

Their life began with joy. Years of happiness shrouded the beloved duo as they heaped their time and money on New Orleans and the area surrounding it. **House** radiated kindness and peace to all.

# ELEVEN: THE FUNERAL

Sweet cerulean-hued days slowly cascaded past. The beautiful *White House* lovingly shrouded two people within the boundaries of the land that they loved. Seldom, did the couple leave the borders and seldom did others visit them. Their love for each other was enough. **House** did not enjoy guests. Special events within New Orleans may tempt a night out now and then, but most of their time gently trickled past inside the gates surrounding **House**. Steven enjoyed sunning by the lake and pool on long, hot summer days. Clarissa devoted hours of her time with a paint brush in hand. Several murals of soft pastel hues delighted the couple from the shiny white walls. **House** skillfully became enveloped within the stories of the New Orleans area. Often, neighbors knocked at the gate as they heard the sobering tales of historical importance displayed on the walls of this grand home. The staff told many outsiders of the artistic craft which the new Mrs. Hinckley possessed. No welcome did they extend to the hopeful visitors. It wasn't that the couple meant to be rude. They were just selfish with their time. Each day was a gift from God. Especially Clarissa felt the flight of the minutes. Steven's age scared her. She did not desire to be a widow. Her love for her husband was profound and real. Fear frequently pulled at her heart. What would she do if her beloved should die first? Perhaps a morbid thought, but it was hers.

Eventually, Steven joined Clarissa in her story skillfully displayed with love and paint on the interior's glistening surfaces. As the walls of **House** filled with lavish, strokes of layers of paint, stories of local lore continued to grace the white walls. Especially beautiful were tales of the Gautier family history. One day, Mr. Hinckley announced that he desired to paint beside his wife. He never knew of the talent which ebbed through his veins. How could he suddenly paint with such precision and skill? It seemed impossible that one, without lessons, could paint with such ease. **House** demanded more and more of their time. She must make sure that they did not tire of her confinements, which precipitated the need to create a desire for the man who once spent time on the golf course now to embrace painting.

Time began to rush past as he lovingly stroked green onto the alabaster walls. Clarissa agreed that his skill seemed magically to increase very quickly. Hours, days, weeks, and months progressed into years as joyful laughter echoed from the bright murals. The couple's joy delighted the staff. Most had never witnessed such love. The stories spread throughout the area of a love so real and intense. **House** determined that this particular couple would enjoy their final days. Yes, time was almost over for the two.

Lately, Clarissa noticed a slowness in Steven. Her love did not appear bright and energized as usual. They had painted late into the night. The next morning, he appeared confused. He must be tired. She insisted that he go to the pool and relax for a while. Her intention to join him quickly was forgotten as she continued her current story on the wall. Hours passed. Steven never came to view her work which was strange. Frequently, they forgot to eat lunch. That was not unusual, but always they were together. Finally, as twilight beckoned the end of the day, she realized that the day passed without Steven's usual interruptions.

Instantly, with this realization, she hastened to the pool. Her beloved was floating on top of the water. Steven's head bobbed on the surface. She ran into the warm wetness and pulled him toward her. Screams of terror caused

Cook to run out. Steven had been dead for hours. Members of the staff carried his blue, withered body to the side of the pool. Clarissa continued to howl and pull him to her chest.

The staff phoned Dr. Simmons to check on the hysterical wife. He finally had to inject a sedative into her arm. Members of the staff sat by her bed. The staff did not summon any of their friends. The couple no longer had friends. Darkness filled *Joyful*. There was no longer joy in those long, dark halls. No visitors came to help care for the widow Hinckley. Alone, Clarissa stood by the grave of the man who filled her past twenty years with happiness. Tears fell. She was unaware that only their staff attended the funeral. It was unimportant. They buried him as he had lived, only loved by one. Clarissa tried to remain in *Joyful*. Her desire was to finish her time on earth completing the murals which once brought her such contentment. Such a goal did happen. She died two months after her husband, alone in a chair by the last mural he completed.

The staff again attended the funeral of the one they loved. No others came. Fittingly, Clarissa found peace buried beside the love of her life. The people, who were like members of their family, quietly left the halls where they worked for other homes and families. Never would they forget joy and happiness which abounded at the beautiful *White House*. Neighbors drove past the locked gates with sad hearts for the two who only desired time with each other.

## TWELVE: JAKE AND JASMINE

**House** no longer gleamed. The beloved handyman continued to care for her but not to the extent as when she contained owners. Two years passed since the death and burial of the Hinckley couple. As she weathered the storms of life alone, sadness filled the darkened space of **House.** Locals slithered into the gates. Here they drank by the once pristine waters. Empty beer cans now floated on the dark green, polluted waters of the pool. **House** looked her age. No plastic surgery was provided to restore her fading beauty.

On a bright August day, a real estate agent drove inside her gates. The agent bubbled with joy at the hefty commission she might score should she unload the property. This young agent arrived early to open the drapes and spruce up the interior if only superficially. **House** despised the phony who flitted around her elegant interior.

"Well, **House** looks like you may soon have new owners."

Under her breath, she hissed, "How ridiculous these rumors are that this house understands what you say, little on what you think. This big, ole white elephant no longer is so beautiful. Her value is nothing to what it once attained. Sad, that it has fallen into such disrepair."

Cruelly, the woman pulled a piece of peeled paint from the once shiny walls. **House** hated hypocrites. This person, Lisa, was one of the worst in New Orleans. She would do anything for a commission. **House** stood majestically by the lake as this person rushed around doing meaningless tasks trying to score a sale. If she had maintained the property, with the funds set aside, instead of embezzling them, **House** could have remained regale.

On time, a shiny gray Cadillac drove inside the gates. **House** watched as a handsome couple walked onto her large, front porch. The man was a Naval graduate from Annapolis. Recently retired from over twenty years of service, his reputation was sterling. Jake possessed a handsomeness which was startling. He stood over six foot three inches which made him tower over all the previous owners. Brown hair with emerald green eyes caused most women to swoon. **House** felt a little wobbly as he sauntered inside.

Jasmine, a petite young woman, possessed brown hair with large coper-colored eyes. Her skin was something to behold. Silky texture the color of golden honey, she turned heads wherever she traveled. **House** hoped these beautiful people appreciated her beauty despite a slightly run-down appearance.

Quietly, they followed Lisa around the grounds as she gushed expletives and pointed out details they noticed long before her ravings. If only the idiot real estate agent would shut up and let them digest what they witnessed.

Suddenly, Jake quietly announced, "We want to purchase the home."

His smile melted the agent into the floor. She hinted and hawed but hastily produced a contract. They all sat at the dining room table as they worked out wording that pleased them.

"Mr. Jones, I'm surprised that you didn't discuss this with the little wife." She looked condescendingly at Jasmine and smiled her hypocritical smile.

"Oh, we discussed our decision for days. You see, we knew when we phoned you that we would purchase this beautiful estate." **House** smiled.

"We were friends with Steven and Lorraine Hinckley's kids. We enjoyed a party or two here. This place is such a lovely, old southern home. We can't imagine anyone not appreciating her beauty. They must be foolish, don't you think?" **House** glowed.

"Yes, of course, you are correct. I've always thought this was the prettiest place in the entire state of Louisiana.

This house can understand you. Did you know that?"

Lisa watched in horror as a rogue bee swooped down on her. In a hurry to show property and possibly write a contract, she had forgotten her Epi-Pen. The bee landed on her lip with a powerful sting. Her scream made even **House** shutter.

Poor Lisa was declared dead by the time the ambulance arrived. Jake and Jasmine looked at each other with understanding. "I guess Lory and Ted were correct about our home. You better be attractive and stylish to win her affection. I'm glad that we have filled the bill. We are sorry Lisa, but you were not a real person."

Jake kissed his gorgeous wife.

"Welcome home, my beauty."

## THIRTEEN: THE MONSTER

Jake and Jasmine Jones moved into **House**, a place which they once admired at a much younger age.
"You know, Jas, I never dreamed that someday we might live here." He stretched his long, muscular arms to encompass the area with a sweeping gesture.
Jasmine only smiled. Lazily, they relaxed by the azure waters of the meandering pool. Jake studied his gorgeous wife with interest. She was almost perfect. There was this small freckle on the back of her leg which irritated him. He searched through many women to find a perfect specimen, one worthy of his stunning body. This handsome soldier possessed a beauty of undefined perfection. Married now for over six months, his new bride pleased him, except for that freckle on the backside of her leg. Once, he suggested that they visit a plastic surgeon, but

Jasmine said it was not possible to remove the brown spot so he tried not to bring it up. Not only was his wife fragile in body but her spirit was weak.

Each day, he became more annoyed by her weakness and that freckle. It was the only thing that registered as he watched her sway down the stairs in front of him. The fact that her legs were perfectly shaped and draped with golden skin, the color of thick honey, did not matter. Just that freckle seemed to glare at him.

As they sunned by the pool, the small brown spot appeared to grow into a monstrosity. Sweetly, he smiled at her. Her questioning look meant she wondered why he stared at her. His penetrating looks always made her nervous. Many times, he had mentioned the freckle to her. The beauty tried to cover it with make-up, but nothing seemed to help. Lovingly, she stroked his hand. It was, after all, only a freckle. Suddenly, he withdrew his hand from her touch. Sadly, she pushed her sunglasses back over her eyes.

From the beginning of their relationship, she knew that she could never please him. Other women told her about encounters with the valiant young officer. He demanded perfection. His twenty years of service to his country had created a disciplined machine. Slowly, she watched him become undone right before her brown eyes of love and devotion. Jasmine would do anything for Jake. If only he wasn't such a perfectionist and could ease up a little on her flaws.

Sometimes, her love frightened her with his looks of disdain. What was he thinking? Was she paranoid? Early, in their relationship, he told her how perfect they were for each other. Only she could make him happy. Now, they owned the most spectacular home in Louisiana. Still, he found fault with her and did not appear truly happy. They needed a baby. Surely, that was the answer! Maybe then he would concentrate on the gift of the perfect child. Jake refused to discuss having children. He declined to discuss it, so she patiently waited. Answering his every call, she attempted to keep him happy.

Three years passed for the almost perfect couple. On their third anniversary, Jake noticed that his wife had gained a little weight. While they sunned by the lake, he observed her as she napped in the bright sunshine. Yes, she had a little bump in her stomach. Rage consumed him. Did she defile his wishes? Some of his friends told how their wife miraculously became pregnant while on the pill. He would laugh with glee at their admissions. The bitch must think that they were idiots. Now, was he about to experience that very scenario? Jasmine lazily stretched a long cat-like pull on her muscles. She yawned unaware that her beloved was watching. Out of nowhere, the chair lifted high in the air. The chaise lounge, on which she relaxed, was hurled into space. With a loud thud, she landed into the deep waters of *Clarissa's Lake.* Jake had promised to change the sign to *Jasmine's Property.*

Her beautiful hairstyle, which she paid a great deal at the best salon in New Orleans, was a mess as she surfaced with water inside her nose and her lungs. The two had made reservations at a premier restaurant in New Orleans with a night away from home to celebrate their third year wedding anniversary. She staggered from the waters while shock consumed her with she realized that Jake threw her into the water. His spot beside her now was empty. Scared and unsure of what happened, she stumbled back onto her chair. Gently, tears ran down her cheeks. Her greatest fear presented itself. Hadn't her father begged her not to marry this soldier who served his country on some of the most dangerous missions in the world? Tears streamed from eyes of deepest brown. Happy eyes now scarred with fear and uncertainty of what the future held for her.

Jake stood inside by the sink. He sipped his beer and watched Jasmine. Yes, he understood her thought process. She tried to make sense of his actions. The large man bowed his head.

"Please don't start. For years, I have hidden my anger. It has not dissipated as I had hoped. Never would I have married that beautiful woman if I knew this monster was about to surface again." He said these words almost silently to himself. **House** listened sadly. Memories of similar moments came to the soldier's mind. Women of exquisite beauty whom he quickly found repulsive because of some small flaw. Why could he not find a perfect girl? He, after all, was perfect. Wasn't it strange that he found himself without reproach, but all women eventually failed him? Faces paraded before his mind: broken noses, red swollen eyes, purple lips large and cracked from his slaps which progressed to punches. Each time, he promised that it would never happen again. Jewelry accompanied by his vows of sorrow humbly he thrust at the feet of his victim. He was forgiven over and over until the sorrowful creature finally accepted the fact that he could not change.

Jasmine was the love of his life. If only that freckle would disappear and her weight gain explained to him, someday, he would father a child with her. His baby must be the perfect specimen, just like him.

Again, he watched Jasmine struggle with her emotions outside in the fading light. It was all standard procedure. The couple should be on their way to the city for a celebration.

Jake walked up the grand staircase. In their bedroom on the top of the shelf, hidden in the very back, he removed a small mahogany box. Caressingly, the soldier opened the lid. With such care, he removed it. The thing which he hid because his feelings for it were confused. Once, it gave him pride and affirmation of how special he was. With time, he hated it. The soldier held the Medal of Honor up to the late light of day. How many other lives had this token of love and respect stolen from this great country? How many other monsters had been created to hold this small emblem of bravery only to wish that they never had to do the actions required? It wasn't his actions on the battlefield that pulled at his emotions. He would repeat any or all of those. It was the brutal assault of innocent, young women who were only guilty of loving him. For some reason, he felt out of control in every relationship. They all began filled with love but eventually, he snapped. That killing machine, which was needed to survive on the battlefield, could not be harnessed into coping with normal life. His mind told him, it wasn't his fault. The problem was with everyone else. They contained flaws. He knew well the scenario about to be played out with Jasmine. He would contain the anger and rage for as long as possible, but it would assault her.

His inability to stop his madness had a reason. Thoughts of a distant house in a foreign country controlled his mind. He could feel the dry heat. The horrible discomfort made worse by his fatigues. Distant bombings caused the ground to move. It was all unbearable but must be borne with courage. One must be courageous. Jake was a Navy Seal. The finest of those worthy to wear the medals he possessed. Horrible things were required of these men. Unspeakable actions to stop those without morals or ethics from harming the country that they loved.

Hate faced Jake daily while he fought from eyes without a heart. Hate which consumed the soul of that other soldier, his enemy. Jake must annihilate them. It was clear: Kill or be killed. The killing wasn't painful for him. He was a trained assassin. The hard thing was that it destroyed something inside him. Yes, he was capable of love and tenderness but underneath that was an uncontrollable rage. It became easy to snap a neck or thrust a knife into the soft flesh of an enemy. It was just as easy now to yell and rant at the weak. Sometimes, in his mind, they were the same.

Jake walked to one of the guest rooms and closed the door. What a room of softness greeted him, soft white with a slight green tint reflected the late streaks of sunlight through the plantation shutters. He carefully touched the silk duvet. Was this one of the rooms which Jasmine redecorated? He couldn't remember. Thoughts of Jasmine always made him smile. So small in statue yet paramount in his heart, he had never loved any woman as much as he loved her. It wasn't too late. She would forgive him many, many times before he ruined it. He needed to pull this maniac back into the shackles of his mind. It would be possible for a while to make their love endure. Eventually, he would lose her love. With remorse, he turned on the shower and cried.

**House** felt sorrow for this man of beauty. Jake was not just beautiful on the outside, but also so valiant inside. At least, for a time he was. Scarred by demands of battle, the rage sometimes was impossible to contain. **House** loved him for she also understood the emotion of uncontrollable rage. The parallel wasn't just with the feeling of anger but the search for perfection. **House** loved Claire, Clarissa, and Jake because of the beauty and style which they possessed. They were perfect. Just the same, she felt repulsed by Lorraine and her squeaky voice. As she had been by the mousy real estate agent, Lisa, with her bad complexion, horrible wardrobe, and hypocritical ways. Yes, perfection was a brutal thing.

# FOURTEEN: LIFE GOES ON

Weak? Really? Jasmine stayed by the pool for about one hour. Sadly, she packed up her things and walked inside. They should have been enjoying their favorite restaurant in New Orleans. One of their favorite rooms at the Roosevelt Hotel had been reserved. It sat empty, waiting for them. She would not call to cancel the reservation because she no longer cared. Those things seemed trivial. What was the point of worrying over reservations? She and her handsome husband may never enjoy a meal or an evening out together ever again. Why should she care if she phoned a restaurant that she would never frequent again with Jake?

When she entered the bedroom, it was a shock that he wasn't there. The other car remained in the garage, so he had not left. Quietly, she walked down the hall. One of the guest rooms had a closed door. Silently, she approached. The door was locked. That was good. Tomorrow, they would discuss what happened. Now, she needed to plan her day tomorrow when she would leave him. She walked into her bedroom and kneeled by the bed. Extreme sadness and fatigue plunged her into a deep moroseness. She prayed for guidance. If she had done anything to provoke the man whom she loved, she had no clue what it was. All through the night, she cried and prayed for guidance. Their survival depended on what occurred tomorrow.

Weak? Really? The person who arose the next morning was not delicate. Jasmine emerged with resolve and determination. She had thought last night about packing her bags and just leaving but decided to wait.

Jasmine dressed for the day and bounded down the stairs. Not an inch of sadness did she display. After praying last night, she turned the problem over to God. Now, they were in His hands.

Surprise shocked her with the realization that Jake was preparing breakfast. He had never done that before. Without hesitation, she boldly walked into the sunny, white kitchen. All of the cabinets were a silky white with white marble counter tops. The bright sun bounced off the surfaces. She always felt amazed at the beauty of the kitchen which Claire designed. A small sign hung over the kitchen sink; *This is Claire's Kitchen.* Jake had promised to make a new sign proclaiming *Jasmine's Galley.* She guessed that would not occur now.

"Well, good morning, sunshine. Did you sleep well? I slept like a drunken sailor."

She looked at him in amazement.

"Let me get this straight. You threw me into the lake, and now you are my cheery husband again? I don't think so. After breakfast, I'll pack my things and be out of your way. Never, will that happen to me again. How dare you?"

Against her resolve, tears flowed from her eyes, but she managed not to lose

herself entirely. The petite woman walked to the cabinet and filled her favorite Blue Willow cup with the finest coffee sold in New Orleans. She glared at Jake. This morning, in the bright sunlight, she wasn't afraid of him even though he towered over her small frame.
"Yes, I know. I remember well my outrageous actions last night. A while ago, I phoned the hotel and restaurant. We are on for tonight. Why don't we have a quick breakfast and leave for the city? We'll spend the day just meandering in your favorite stores. There is a small but expensive gift waiting for you in the finest jewelry store." He kissed her gently on the cheek and wiped her tears away with his manly hand. She was bewildered by his actions.

"I don't think so. Men who throw women into lakes are of no interest to me. I'm going to pack and visit my dad. He has never even raised his voice at me. I'll be out of your way as soon as I have my coffee."

The smell of bacon frying in the pan and fresh banana pancakes heaped on a platter with hot syrup covered in melted butter presented a real problem for her. Neither had eaten last night. She was starving. Jasmine may be small, but her appetite was great.

Jake knew her needs and counted on that very thing to save him. He heaped a hefty serving of bacon and pancakes onto a plate with a generous slab of butter and hot syrup topping. Her tiny frame demanded small, frequent feedings but if she missed a meal, she became ravenous. Her mouth salivated at the delightful aromas. The coffee was excellent.

Without planning on it, she plopped into a chair at the breakfast table and dived into the feast. Jake smiled. Maybe the way to a man's heart was through his stomach, but that may be the case for women as well.

He served himself and sat by her side. No one spoke for the longest time. Carefully, he hooked his index finger into her left hand. Reflexes caused her hand to close around his. He smiled. She seemed unaware of her actions. Quickly, she rose for a second serving. The breakfast was hot and delicious. Silently the two sat side by side and consumed a meal as if they had no problems in the world.

"Look; Jasmine, I know that my behavior was despicable. Just know that I am beside myself with disappointment in my actions. I lied earlier when I stated that I had slept like a 'drunken sailor.' Actually, I barely slept at all."

If he told the truth, he slept like a baby. Not a problem crossed his mind. He was a master at mending his messes. She was good for several rounds before leaving him. He had time to change his abusive ways although he doubted that he ever could. The Navy created what they needed to win wars. It was up to him to automatically join the rest of the world when his time as a soldier was completed. His problem was that he was an excellent warrior. He had no experience as a husband. How did he figure this out and kill the raging bull inside?

These thoughts caused him to stop talking and reflect. Jasmine looked at the good-looking man sitting by her side. Jake was not handsome; he was beautiful. His towering frame only made him seem more human and vulnerable at the moment. It was impossible for the average person to understand the demands placed on these trained fighters. She was aware of the impossibility of his situation. He loved her. That was a fact. No one spoke. The sound of the ticking clock over the sink reminded them that time was running past.

Without speaking, she took his hands. The greenest eyes in the world looked sadly into her soul. They seemed to beg forgiveness and another chance. Even though he spoke no words, she nodded at him.

"Our bags are still packed. Let's leave the mess for Millie. She won't mind." Jake scooped her into his arms. Laughing gaily, they grabbed their luggage and left for a night or two in the city. They never mentioned the entire episode again. Jake smiled as he considered that he had at least five more similar bouts before Jasmine would leave. Surely, he could repair himself.

**House** shuddered as they closed the door.

"They are doomed. I'll be left alone again." **House** silently waited for their return.

## FIFTEEN: JAKE'S BATTLE

He tried, Jake worked every day, to pull the monster inside his soul. Jasmine had no idea of the horrendous battle which raged in his heart and mind. The small woman with brown hair and eyes could not have been more loved by the large man with eyes the color of old emeralds. He laughed at her jokes. They had sex as always. There did not appear anything strange in his behavior. Any possibility that she may realize the broken man before her silently faded each day. In fact, years passed. Occasionally, he would get angry. Once, he threw a plate at something that she said. Small things which did not seem important to her at the time. Each instance that his anger loosened itself from his shackles, he shook with dread that it had finally broken free. Lurking deep inside was something waiting. Silently, this deformity sat like cancer waiting for the day when the metastasis could begin.

When it did occur, there was no reeling it back into his core. Jake would be powerless.

**House** suspected that something broke in this man. The vibrations emitted from his emotional structure did not seem reasonable. This situation was unlike anything that **House** had experienced. Yes, **House** knew how to detect stupid or annoying behavior, but this was something else. **House** continued to support the couple. However, Claire was the one, the only one really whom **House** pined for each day. If only she could bound back inside the glistening white walls.

Memories, such wonderful memories flowed from the past years. There had been other residents who made **House** laugh, but no one could touch the deep yearning which consumed **House** for that blond beauty with the large, blue eyes. Babe was the exact image of her mother. If not Claire, then the structure could be fulfilled with the presence of the younger version of the woman whom she loved. Life with the Gautier family had filled time with ease and pleasantries. There was no unrequited anger lurking in those souls. What loomed here, in the present, presented fear.

Jake and Jasmine appeared real. They laughed. Love was pledged daily, and they made love in the bed they shared, but something was missing. Robots, they seemed programmed and predictable. That is until the day that Jasmine made a terrible mistake. It seemed innocent. Certainly, it was nothing which should have created what resulted. Poor Jasmine, she had been marked from the day that she let this handsome man into her heart. Each day, which passed after her heart was bound to his, ticked forward as a bomb waiting for detonation. She could not have known the peril that waited for her. No one, not even **House,** could predict the horror about to occur.

Jake had slept restlessly that night. He experienced flashbacks from a particularly horrific event during his time in the Navy Seals. During the evening, the soldier awoke with a splitting headache. Finally, unable to sleep, he arose to find something for the pain. Seldom did he take medication. He feared what may occur if he medicated himself. Jasmine had some pain medicine. He took two. Swallowing them rapidly, he only wanted sleep. She awakened to see her gorgeous husband standing in the moonlight which streamed through the shutters. His large, green eyes seemed to glow. Softly, she groaned. Jake shook his head.

"Not tonight, Jasmine, I'm not sleeping. I must get rest."

She laughed her gentle, soft laugh. "Maybe I have just the thing to tire you."

He shook with anger at her when, out of the blue, she climbed on top of him. Her actions surprised Jake, for finally, he had started to relax. Anger flooded throughout his mind. How dare she be the aggressor?

*What has happened to my sweet, little wife?*

Unaware of the strength which overtook him, he shoved her hard onto the floor. The small woman felt humiliated. Jasmine's head hit the floor with a loud thud. Wails screamed from her very heart.

"What is wrong with you? You are never interested in me. Don't you love me anymore? What has happened to us?" Jake raged as he loomed over her crumpled form which pulled in the fetus position on the floor. The cancer had been released. There was no pulling back the monster. He hated weakness. Tears and whining did not soften him. Those actions made him harder and angrier.

"No, I don't love you, Jasmine. In fact, I detest you. Your very presence creates the desire for me to run. My desire is to run as far from you as I possibly can." Poor Jasmine only screamed louder and reached toward him in desperation. That was the action which precipitated the end. More than all emotions, the trained warrior hated desperation. In his training, there was no room for such a response. His training dictated that he must make rapid decisions and stand by the consequences. Desperation did not exist, not in his playbook.

Jake grabbed her from the floor. Over and over, he shook her as if she was a doll. No longer did she react with desperation; only silence filled the moderately lit room.

After shaking her for so long, he threw her onto the floor. Blood smeared on her face and nightgown. He had not noticed that she was bleeding earlier. Horror filled his heart. Large hands, which once gently held her small frame, now were fearful of touching the broken figure. Also broken were all of their dreams and plans. No tears fell from the emerald eyes. He found it impossible to remember the last time that he cried. Instead, he sat by her side and sung a lullaby that his mother once used to soothe his childish fears.

Hours ticked past on the hall clock. **House** trembled not just for the beautiful, damaged Jasmine but Jake. He would never recover from this. Softly, **House** swayed in the wind. A storm blew in from the direction of Lake Pontchartrain. Lightning threw bolts of light around the quiet bedroom. Thunder roared so loudly that the gentle song from the lips of Jake diffused.

**House** knew what action must be taken. Jake would never survive institution. For a warrior to be locked away from the glories of nature while he was forced to live in bondage would be unbearable. **House** must save him from a fate worse than death. Jake found it impossible not to stroke Jasmine. Now, blood not only covered her face but his as well. He tasted the blood from her which covered his hands. Soon, his face covered with the dark red, sticky liquid.

Time ticked past. When an unusually loud boom ricocheted and the lightning flashed as daylight, **House** moved so hard on her foundation that she pulled free from the electrical wires deep in the basement. Sparks flew at the break in the electrical current. Jake looked up at the ceiling.

"**House**, I always knew that you were alive. Take me away from this pain. I can't live without her."

He bowed his head and waited for **House** to set him free from his tormented life.

She did just that as several electrical fires throughout the New Orleans area resulted from the massive, turbulent storm. One of them consumed the bedroom of the beautiful *White House* which was also named, *Claire's House*. Due to the number of fires from the massive storm, a firetruck passed the house as the orange and red flames glowed in the bedroom upstairs. Immediately, the firefighters turned back to the *White House.* They rammed through the gates and knocked down the door.

Skill from the firemen prevented severe damage to **House**, but the bedroom was a disaster. That room was burned entirely with the bodies of the two owners.

The next owners of *Claire's House* would need a nice bank account to remedy the ruinous results from fire and water. Not to worry, they waited in the background. It wasn't the money that should have worried them. The bar of excellence set by **House** demanded perfection. This couple was far from that.

## SIXTEEN: BILL BIVENS

Bill Bivens was an uneducated man. His school, which taught him everything, was the school of hard knocks. He was a hard drinking, crude talking, wife beating epitome of his father, Lester. Bill had one thing going for him; he knew the building industry. Although he did not graduate from high school, he learned on the building sites of his father. Lester Bivens was a prolific builder in the New Orleans area. From the Fifth Ward to the Garden District, no house was too small or simple nor too large or complex for his talents.
Lester apprenticed to his father as his father and the father before had done. Bivens Builders had amassed a small fortune. More educated, sophisticated masons marveled at the success of this company of the less educated compared to the years of formal education of most. The Bivens family knew one crucial fact: yes, they did drink hard and

seemed crude, but they were honest and hard working. When they said they would arrive at a scheduled time, they were there earlier than the time agreed. Their word was their bond.

Consequently, they were embraced by the wealthy and not-so-wealthy. Hence, they accumulated a small fortune building dependable homes.

Bill had taken over the company when Lester fell three stories from a job site. His injuries didn't kill him, but he lived in constant pain from his fall. Broken and bent, he could no longer work. His son, Bill, stepped right into his shoes. More than qualified, he supervised each job site. He visited every home site on his work tours. The workers never knew when he might show so they worked as if it might be that day. They would never leave a site without sweeping up their mess and picking up any litter. To leave such a mess would cost them their job. Bill was a master builder.

Claire and Christophe Gautier chose Bivens Builders for their home's construction. The best and most competent hands in the area crafted *Claire's House.* No wonder the design was copied many times.

After the demise of Jake and Jasmine, Bill lovingly hung sheets of plywood over the windows and damaged sides of the fire-ravaged home. Mr. Bivens was the official caretaker of *Claire's House.* From the time it was completed, he promised Christophe that he would always watch over the mansion. His actions resulted in a hefty salary to him from each owner who graced the house after the horrific crash of the Gautier family's plane.

Since Bill maintained the property, after the loss of the first owners, he had patched the uneven pavers after Lorraine's fall. The beautiful murals, which Steven and Clarissa labored over, were kept vibrant and fresh by painters sent each year to make sure the *White*

*House* would sparkle as designed. Exterminators frequented to prevent rogue bees like the one which stung Lisa. Now, sadly, after the fire, this builder made sure that none of the elements could cause further damage to the structure that he lovingly referred to as "my favorite home."

On the day when he had covered all the damaged areas, he sat on a stone bench in the front gardens enjoying his lunch. A navy-blue Jaguar pulled up to the gate. The horn blew, so Bill meandered over. The driver was a single woman.

"I am about to marry the love of my life. Can I look at this beauty? It would please me to present my future husband with this house for a wedding present."

Bill gave a little whistle and shook his head as he opened the gates.

"Wow, must be nice. I must have married the wrong woman. My wife only gave me a headache." He mumbled under his breath.

Mrs. Bivens hated her husband's drinking. They regularly fought about it. Last night, he was forced to knock her to the ground for her ranting about "his problem." The only issue that he recognized was her.

"Sure, come on inside. This place is a beauty if I may say."

Proudly, he explained that he had built this home with a lot of money and even more love.

Enter owner number five, Carolyn and her future husband, Teddy. **House** trembled as she did when she knew this owner would not be agreeable. Wait until **House** saw the "future husband." She would never welcome this couple!

# SEVENTEEN: CAROLYN AND TEDDY

Carolyn felt delighted with her beautiful new home; her excitement burst inside her heart. Accustomed to abuse from her long-time lover, she finally stood on the threshold of her dream. Since her first year of college, her goal was attracting the handsome Teddy. Whenever she gazed on him, she still saw the thin, handsome man back in his college days. He was now thin but not because of healthy choices. Teddy had been a drug abuser since those long-ago college days. Now, drastically gaunt with an angry disposition, the only thing that pleased him was slipping into the drug-induced haze which filled most of his days. Without those halcyon times, his temper exploded. Carolyn consumed most of those treacherous outbursts. Still, she loved the man whom most people ignored.

Two days after the repairs and renovations on **House** were completed, Teddy flew the couple from their home in New York to Carolyn's beach home in Florida where they were married. Her dream fulfilled at last. Joy filled her heart. Teddy, he didn't care about such ridiculous things. His next "score" consumed his thoughts. Carolyn was his enabler and provider. With her large bank account, life looked pretty good to the man whom most labeled as a "loser." Carolyn agreed, over a year ago, to participate in the fun with him. Now, she was addicted to the current drug of choice, heroin.

No one stopped the couple from flying in her private jet. The air controllers turned the other way. This couple was people of privilege and social connections. Still, the plane did not clear until the air space looked safe. If these careless individuals wanted to kill themselves, who cared? As long as no one else went down because of their spoiled existence, good riddance to the stoned couple.

The two staggered to the plane. Teddy blew her a kiss in the air as he started the engine. Carolyn was high but not as much as he. At the moment, he looked absurd to her. Just the same, she smiled, and blew the kiss back to him.

"Before we take off, I need to tell you why we are going to Louisiana. Don't you even care to know? You never ask questions."

She stroked his hand which stained from smoking too much nicotine and weed. He looked blankly at her and waited. As she struggled to find the words, he groaned.

"Please don't tell me that you are going to explain for the hundredth time why no one from your fancy family showed at our wedding. Did you note that the only person there was my beloved brother, Troy? The etiquette and garbage that you constantly spew don't mean much. You know what? It doesn't matter."

He lowered his head. All of her explanations and drama tired him.

"No, I agree. My family is horrible. We will never entertain them at our new home. Remember the beautiful home that I have been describing? Here is the clincher, I purchased the beauty for you. It is all yours, my darling. Now, take us home." Lovingly, she continued to stroke his hand.

"Let me try to comprehend you. Out of all the dumb things which you have done, and there is a great deal, you have purchased a home for me without my seeing it? Are you insane? I have never even mentioned liking Louisiana. You are a loser, Carolyn."

The woman felt his anger begin toward her. It would grow as a plague.

"Oh, let me explain. It is a wedding present for you, my dearest love." Her gushiness angered him even more.

"Let me get this right; you rich people give each other a wedding present? That is the dumbest thing I have ever heard. I married you, didn't I? What more do you want from me? Not only did I not purchase you a 'wedding present' I will never buy anything else for you. I am your gift for life. Does that make you happy?"

He imitated her high voice when he issued the words. Then, laughter erupted from his angry mouth. How many times would she repeat the same actions? She thought of the adage that the sign of insanity was repeating the same action, hoping for a different outcome.

The next words were fatal. The outcome was exactly as everyone who knew the two would have predicted.

"Look, try to be nice. It is our wedding day. Don't be angry and sulk. You are going to love the house."

Those words were the biggest mistake of her life. If there was anything that the druggie hated, it was being told what to

think and feel. Suddenly, he began to taxi down the long runway. Carolyn felt fear. It was bad enough being in the air with a pilot who was compromised in judgment but now she had added anger to the equation; this would not end well.
"Teddy, let's go back. I have forgotten something important. Please turn around and take me back. We'll visit the new home tomorrow."
Without a word, he took off from the security of the ground to the ominous-looking sky. Carolyn clutched the armrest and sighed. What had she done now?
They spoke no words for the longest time. Carolyn studied her new husband. His jaw was set in the firm clinch which meant his anger was growing.
What was it that she found so attractive about him? As if seeing him for the first time in years, she realized the scars of constant drug use. He was not the Teddy of her dreams. Now, she had confined herself to live with him for the rest of

her life. Emotion shook her body. Tears welled in her eyes. Her dreams, now realized, seemed ridiculous. Yes, she finally accomplished her wishes, but she desperately needed to undo this madman's clutches.

"It pleases me to tell you that before I signed my execution papers to marry you, I saw an attorney. All that I own, which happens to be a mansion in Louisiana, now belongs to the love of my life, Susie. You remember my 'drug buddy' Susie? You know, the one who you always despised so much? Now, she will inherit your big ole bayou house." He laughed wickedly as his eyes remained glued to the sky.

"How dare you! Have you left everything to that scant of a woman? You are correct. I detest her whiny voice and inability to control herself. Susie is lazy and a user. Never, will she amount to anything! She will never live in my beautiful home."

Out of nowhere, a blow landed to her right temple. Blood splattered. The frightened woman fell against the window to her right. Her world turned dark but not before she remembered her handsome college man. He had won many trophies for boxing. He had been a legend at Vanderbilt University. The woman's screams assaulted the silence of the cockpit.

Another blow, harder than the first, landed on the right shoulder. It nailed Carolyn into the side of the plane. The last thing that she saw was a jab of tremendous strength leveled dead-straight into her eyes. Blood erupted with force from her nasal cavity and eyes.

Teddy began to rant. "This is your fault. You can't keep your big mouth shut, can you? Now, look at what you have caused. Stop bleeding, right now. Do you hear me? You stop bleeding. Answer me."

He released his grip on the controls of the plane. It began to fly out of control. He grabbed the broken woman and shook her hard. The blood escalated in force.

Suddenly, screams as from a banshee filled the air. Teddy realized the screams were his and that he had finally ended the chapter of their life on earth. It was a sad story of unused talents and squander. He no longer cared if they plummeted from the sky. It was necessary to end the nightmare which they called "life."

The plane continued to plunge toward the ground until it crashed in a bayou of Louisiana. Exactly one mile from the shiny *White House* with dark green shutters. The impact shook the area. **House** trembled from the eruption of fire that burned only briefly. The wrecked plane remained hidden from view; the remains would escape detection for many months.

Was this the action of **House**? Many would say that it was. The *Legend of the*

*Cursed Mansion* began with the crash of Carolyn and Teddy. It would continue for many years. For now, a druggie would inherit an object of great beauty, not from hard work but from the generosity of a woman in love to the man of her dreams. The coming years would prove to be the hardest in the history of **House.**

# EIGHTEEN: **HOUSE**

Poor **House,** why could she not experience the happiness of most homes? She longed for Claire and Babe or at least the lovely Clarissa. Surely, there were other women with grace and style who would fill her chambers with flowers, music, and social events.
**House** desired to find people who would love her, besides Bivens Builders. Sure, Bill did admire **House** but he was the builder, he should love her.
**House** sat day after day waiting to meet the new owners. Carolyn had not impressed the structure, but maybe her husband would have class and style. Briefly, **House** missed Jake. He oozed plenty of sophistication as well as anger. Could she not find happiness in someone who would keep her appearance fresh and pristine? Owners who filled her with pride at their accomplishments and wonderful parties? Days filtered past. Weeks silently

crawled as **House** sat empty and alone. Months seemed to last forever. Finally, one day Bivens drove through the gates. Slowly, he walked toward the beautiful, *La Maison Blanche.*

**House** waited, it would not be good news. She could tell from his gait that he was not happy. What now? Another episode of pain and loss waited. Bill unlocked the front door. He trudged toward the center of the entrance foyer and dropped his keys into a Peretti Thumbprint bowl which Claire purchased at Tiffany's long ago. The shiny red enamel interior usually caused the man to smile but not today. Carefully, he sat on the stairs as he surveyed his proudest accomplishment. "Oh, **House,** why can't you be filled with joy like most other homes?"

**House** sat silently hoping to find the reason that she could not find love. If only the Gautier family would return to her. Why had they never come back to her? Many people walked her halls, but no one discussed the Gautier family. "Claire and Babe loved you. You know that, right **House**?"

Sure, **House** knew that. Finally, Bill told her what happened to the family whom she adored. News of their demise broke something deep inside of the massive building. She sagged a little in her roof. Claire and Babe never returned because they could not. This information was good news! They did not leave her intentionally. That thought had grieved the shiny *White House* for many years now. Yes, **House** killed the young Arthur for his treatment of Coty. Sure, she had caused the death of the Nanny, as well as the demise of the mousy real estate agent, Lisa. That despicable Lorraine placed high demands on everyone but herself. Although lately, Lorraine did not appear unworthy. Still, she upset **House** with her whiny ways. At that point in time, it seemed necessary to destroy the rich, overweight woman. Jake died because of this place of beauty. His death was different. In his case, **House** protected him from a future worse than death. **House** did not cause the plane wreck of Christophe and Claire. How could she? They were the actual holders of the heart of **House.**

**House** waited for more news. If only the builder had shared his story years ago. It would have made a difference to the spirit of *Claire's House.*

"**House,** they say that you caused the death of this latest set of owners. Isn't that sad? The audacity to blame you for the crash of a plane. I know, in my heart, that you are the fault of several deaths. Each of these 'catastrophes' have been investigated by yours truly. None of these deaths should have occurred. I'm on to you. Long ago, when that little boy fell down your stairs, I knew that it wasn't an accident. How do I know these things? I know because I created you. I built you with the finest materials in the world. As you evolved, I loved you. Not only because of your spectacular beauty but because of your heart, your very core of being contains a piece of me."

"**House**, I can't talk to anyone. My wife hates me. She treats me so awful. I have fallen in love with a younger beauty. This young woman is most beautiful. I think that she loves me. Her family is not wealthy. It is a lie, but I told her that I own you. She is a simple woman without a significant amount of intelligence or sophistication like Claire, Babe, and Clarissa. **House**, I'm going to bring her here for a while. Even though I realize that our relationship can't last forever; I will bring her here and make her happy. It breaks my heart to watch her work in the bar where she suffers mistreatment. Men hit on her all day. That's where we met. Her name is Mandy. Please don't hurt her. Let her find joy for a brief time. My wife will find out eventually. That bitch owns my company. So, you see, I can never leave the witch. My hell of a life will never improve except in the stolen time which I will share with Mandy. Please **House,** don't hurt her."

**House** felt sorry for the large man with a mean streak. Where was his meanness at the moment? Bill hung his head and cried. High emotion lifted from his massive shoulders as he sobbed like a child. **House** longed to embrace the man. **House** detested Bivens's wife, Louise. Whenever she stopped by, as **House** rose from the blueprints, she was nasty to her husband. She was bossy and rude to everyone in her path. No wonder the couple fought continuously. Who could life with someone so disagreeable?

Daylight turned to twilight as Bill continued to sob on the grand staircase. Just as the first stars tumbled into the darkened sky, an old car rattled into the gates. A petite woman bounced from the shamble of a vehicle. Gaily, she strutted to the door as if she did not have a care in the world. **House** was not impressed. Mandy's clothes were cheap. Straight from the bins of a warehouse, but they were clean and pressed. Her hair had very dark roots with a peroxide-based drug store hair color. Her looks were not acceptable. **House** sighed. Bill touched her walls lovingly.

"**House,** please show her respect. No, she isn't elegant, but she is a hard worker. No one deserves happiness more than this little woman. I can tell you horror stories about the way that people treat her. Please, just let us love each other here. Within the confines of your arms, let us have just a moment's peace from the throes of pain from Louise and Mandy's husband, Larry. We know it is wrong."

Lovingly, he caressed her walls. This action caused remembrance of Claire and Babe. No one loved her like they. Now, did Bill have the ability to understand her as well as truly provide love? **House** could only hope.

Bill ran to the front door before Mandy could ring the bell. He opened the door with great speed. The small woman threw her tiny arms around his neck. As she pulled him into her body, she looked past the partially opened door.

"Bill, you live here? This house is the most gorgeous place on earth. You mean that we can meet here, in your other home? What about your wife? If Louise finds us, she will go berserk. Are you sure it is safe to meet here?"

Bill gently pulled her inside.

"Welcome to our love nest, Mandy. When you enter this door, you never have to worry about Larry or Louise. You only need to be happy and let me care for you. Never, are you to work or fuss over this place. I have a maid who does all of the work."

He smiled at the slip of a woman. Another lie, but he would hire a maid tomorrow to keep the entire residence polished and clean for her.

He continued to explain that he built the house many years ago but recently purchased it back from an older owner. Why did he lie to her? He didn't need to do that. Mandy wanted desperately to believe him but knew that his words were false.

**House** trembled slightly. Why did Bivens lie to a woman whom he seemed to love? That poor lady would have accepted the truth. It didn't matter to her if he owned **House**. The important thing to her was that he cared for her. True, it was his desire to be good to her and allow her time away from a desperate life of abuse and work but why lie? Why did people lie and deceive each other? **House** knew, at that moment, that she would protect these unhappy folks even if they were committing a deceptive action.

"Here we go again," **House** whispered.

The lovebirds looked at each other with alarm.

"What was that? Did you feel the house tremble? I'm pretty sure that I did." Mandy looked around the hall with big eyes.

"Come upstairs with me. Let me take all of your doubts and fears away. Here, you are safe for as long as you desire to be with me. I sincerely hope that is a long time."

**House** trembled again. "It won't be for long," She sadly whispered.

## NINETEEN: BILL AND MANDY

Louise noticed the change in her husband immediately. Her verbal assaults and insults appeared to slip off his skin. He smiled constantly. Several times, she thought she heard him whistle, *What's Love Got To Do With It?* Had he finally lost his mind?
Her intention, for many years, had been to drive him insane so that she could institutionalize him and sell his company. Back at the beginning, when they did share love, she had persuaded him to put the building company in her name. A terrible mistake for him but one which she held over his head daily. Now, he could never leave her without losing half of everything he owned. Yes, she was indeed smart.
Nothing she did seemed to get a rise from her husband. Time passed without a confrontation from him. He had even stopped drinking lately. Had he started going to church? That was the only thing

which could cause such results. Louise shook her head at the bear of a man. Mandy's husband, Larry, also saw a drastic change in his wife. No longer did she complain about her job at the bar and the fact that he remained unemployed most of the time. His constant stealing prevented him from finding another position due to his police record. He passed his time tinkering with his old truck. Life sure had improved lately. His hag of a wife was bearable.

Neither partner cared what had happened to their mate. It was the change that resulted in happiness for them that mattered.

Mandy explained to Larry that she had signed up for longer hours at the bar. By doing this, she followed the instructions of her new lover, Bill Bivens. Instead, he paid her graciously so that there would be no need for her to work. Mandy rushed to the *White House* now instead of the bar for a time of fancy meals delivered by the best restaurants in the area. Bill surrounded her with roses and candy. Never, in her life, had she experienced such doting and care. Consistently, she pinched herself to see if this was real.

Bill felt like a school boy. He lived for the time with the lovely Mandy. Laughter, flowers, music, and fun filled **House** just as she always desired. Such a happy environment made **House** feel young like when Claire and Christophe ran down her halls so long ago. Life was pleasant, at least for a while.

Things felt normal, so the couple slipped into complacency. Soon, they began to spend long weekends in New Orleans's finest hotels. Elegant restaurants welcomed them. Mandy visited the best salons; her hair glistened with health and vitality at last from the products available in high dollar studios. She appeared polished and elegant instead of rough around the edges. Bill helped her select expensive clothes. He even began to wear high dollar designer casual wear. *Why save the money for Louise to squander?* He asked himself. Yes, life was more than good, times were happy at last. The couple enjoyed the "Good Life." They truly were happy.

Each of their spouses questioned these changes but refused to address the situation. They both were delighted to have peace at home for a change.

Bill encouraged Mandy to spend her days at **House** so that she could relax and sleep later. These times alone at **House** thrilled the young woman. She would dance to the music on the sound system or lie by the pool nude while she sunbathed. These were the happiest times of her young life.

On a sunny day, as she slept by the lake, a car entered the gates of the *White House*. The driver sat quietly taking in the scene before her. Louise shook her head. What was Bill up to now? Indeed, he couldn't afford this place. She had

thought that he finally suffered enough from her abuse and was about to divorce her. Louise smiled. There was no chance that Bill Bivens could afford to live here. He made a great living but had amassed tremendous debt with leverages. What was going on?
A friend of Louise followed him one day after she spied Bivens enjoying lunch with a lovely, younger woman. She followed the two. They
led her to the gates of the *White House.* Carey couldn't wait to share her news with her best friend, Louise.
Mrs. Bill Bivens now sat in her car watching that very house. One thing was clear; Bill did not live here. Carrey must be mistaken. Not knowing what else to do, Louise sneaked around the house. When she witnessed the beautiful woman naked by the lake, she stopped. This young girl was the exact copy of the person her friend had described seeing earlier with Louise's husband. Her antenna rose. At that moment, she

understood. Old Bill was having an affair. The laugh escaped her mouth. Quickly, she jumped behind the wall of the house. After waiting a few minutes, she peeked around the side of the home. The young woman arose with a look of confusion. Probably, the laugh had awakened her, but she was unable to know what had occurred.

Mandy pulled a cover over her body and staggered inside **House**. Her intention was to shower and snuggle down for a nap. The intense heat outside had created exhaustion in her. Yawning, she walked to the fridge for cold water. The chimes echoed down the hall. The young woman froze. No one had ever come to "their" home before. What was she to do? Bill never instructed her as to what action she should take if visitors arrived. For the longest time, she remained frozen with her right hand on the door handle of the refrigerator. No one could see her.

Someone pressed the chimes over and over. The noise became intrusive. Anger swept over Mandy. Who would be so rude? She stomped to the door and opened it quickly. There stood Louise smiling.

"May I come inside? I am friends with the man who owns this home. Are you his wife?" Louise was hateful and mean-spirited.

"Yes, I am Mrs. Bill Bivens. You are?" What a mistake! She couldn't have said a dumber thing. Louise pushed past her and entered the mansion.

"Isn't your husband a builder? I don't think that he can afford a place like this for you. You are his mistress, not his wife. I know this because you see, I am his wife. My name is Louise Bivens. You are?"

Mandy felt sick. All of the joy which they shared was now over. Bill would be furious at her for being naive. The woman collapsed onto the floor and began to cry. Rage overcame Louise.

**House** watched the scene unfold unable to decide what action was needed. Louise pulled Mandy from the floor and struck her hard on the right side of the face. No one could have prepared for the avalanche of hits and kicks from the larger, older woman. She yelled hateful expletives at the younger woman.

"You slut, you will pay for this. You and my slime bag of a husband will both pay. When I finish, he won't own a paper bag. Your name will be trashed. Everyone will know that you are a bitch, home wrecker."

On and on the abuse poured onto Mandy. The poor girl covered her face with small arms and groaned with each blow which was powerfully delivered. Bill, who was working, thought of his beautiful love. He had decided to pick up her favorite Chinese meal as a surprise for their scheduled lunchtime. The builder carried another treat. Nestled in his left pocket was a bright red velvet box. Yes, after months of indecision, he realized that he couldn't live without Mandy in his life. He would rather lose his company to the witch Louise than live without the woman that he truly loved. He pulled into the drive filled with joy. In less than a minute, joy turned to horror when he noticed his wife's car parked in the drive.

Louise was overweight and mean. Quickly, she could decimate Mandy. He ran to the door. It was not locked. When he entered, he screamed. His wife stood over the collapsed, crumpled body of his beautiful love. Louise looked at him with fear.

"Bill, please help me. What have I done? When I figured out that you were having an affair with this slut, I couldn't help it. Now, I know that I love you. I have always loved you. We just went through a difficult time. All marriages do that. Please give me a hand. We will lose not only everything that you worked for but each other. I will spend the rest of my days making this up to you. Please, help me."

She fell onto the floor beside the girl's body in a tearful heap.

**House** watched this scene. Out of all of the deceits and betrayals, this one would go down as the worst. To **House's** amazement, Bill closed and locked the door. Slowly, he walked toward his wife and dead lover. Silently, he looked from one to the other in confusion. This decision would frame his life forever. He quickly studied three options: call the authorities and report the death of Mandy. He could help Louise cover up the murder. Or he could do nothing and let Louise deal with her blunder. He stood quietly observing the episode in shock.

"How do you propose that I help you, Louise? You have done it now."

His wife felt a ray of hope. She couldn't believe that he would even consider helping her. It was urgent that her response be confident and quick.

"You know the history of this house. Everyone knows that there are tales of murder within these walls. Let's make it look like **House** killed her. No one would be surprised, not with the history involving this place."

**House** felt betrayed by the very man who had created her. How could he blame this on the house which he built from the ground? No, he would never help Louise. **House** was sure.

"Louise, I am torn as to what to do. I despise you, but nothing that I do will bring that woman back to me." Bill pointed at the small, bloody body.

He collapsed onto the small frame of Mandy. Tearfully, he pulled her into his arms and rocked her as if she was a child. Blood seeped onto his clothes. Nothing mattered but the indescribable grief which filled his soul. Moments passed. **House** knew that he would either call the police or walk away. Instead, he carried Mandy's body into the garage. Louise followed unsure of what he was doing.

"You are right. If I have lost Mandy, I have nothing left. I won't live with you, but I'll help you. There isn't any reason for all of us to be destroyed. Just don't ever ask me for anything ever again. The garage door is loose. Several workers have looked at it. We decided that we should replace it weeks ago."

Bill gently laid the small body under the massive door. Pulling a ladder under the motorized unit, he took a large hammer and hit the door over and over. It shook mightily before dropping onto the bloody body. Bill couldn't have planned it any more perfectly. Within minutes, the loose structure fell onto the small frame laying beneath it.

Bivens covered Mandy's bloody, pulverized body with the large door. The builder instructed Louise to telephone the authorities. Tearfully, she identified herself. Almost incoherently, she explained that she hired Mandy to clean the house for the new owners who were scheduled to arrive any day.

The authorities never questioned her story. Larry buried his wife. He never knew what really occurred to Mandy. He felt amazed that she had taken an extra job to help with finances. Her burial was a sad spectacle of love from a grieving husband who never showed her the love and devotion she deserved while she lived.

Bill and Louise attended the funeral. Louise put on the show of her life as she rambled. "Mandy's death is my fault. I hired her and left her alone. We knew that there was a problem with the door. I should have instructed her."

Bill shook his head but remained by her side until the episode died down. Then, they sold the company and divided the money. Louise remained in Louisiana. Bill moved to Port St Joe, Florida.

**House** questioned love. Did it even exist?

## TWENTY: THE WORST

The next months would affect **House** in a way never imagined. Teddy's friend, Susie, received word that she was now a wealthy woman, at least in real estate. Carolyn's attorney tracked down the woman who had used drugs since college. Mr. Lambert tried desperately to locate the drifter who lived with anyone who would take her for a few days. Her slovenly ways soon resulted in her being asked to leave everywhere that she landed. Finally, he hired a detective to assist him in locating the woman of new-found wealth.

The detective finally located Susie in Nashville, Tennessee where she had studied years earlier at Vanderbilt University until flunking out. The dirty, and exhausted young woman was located living on the streets.

Mr. Lambert provided transportation for her to New York and paid for a room for two nights so that he would be able to explain to her the new-found wealth which she just received.

Carolyn had loved Teddy; she had since college at Vanderbilt. Now, he had bestowed Carolyn's gift to him onto a woman without a future. Susie's only association, to this family of wealth, was her practice of "using" with Teddy, Carolyn's love.

Sleeping on the street in a run-down alley in Murfreesboro, the young woman was shaken from her halcyon haze by a man hired by the family attorney, Mr. Lambert. The investigator provided clean clothes after she was allowed to shower at a cheap hotel. He handed her bus ticket over begrudgingly. This woman deserved none of these gifts. She had never worked a day in her life. This man, who had three children and a nagging wife, had never received a dime from anyone. His entire life, he worked, and he worked hard.

By the time that she arrived in New York, Susie's mind had cleared somewhat from all of the substance abuse. A taxi took her to a nice hotel. Soon, she began to suffer from withdrawal as her appearance worsened. The sweats and shaking racked her body as did the pain of withdrawal but she suffered alone. Susie was a survivor. Never had this woman seen such luxury as the hotel presented to her. Life was about to get much better for the woman labeled a "loser" since birth.

The next day, she arrived on time at the office of Mr. Lambert, Esquire. The attorney felt disgusted at the waste they forced him to dole-out to someone that his client barely knew. Still, he fulfilled his obligation as kindly as allowed. Susie sipped coffee from Versace China at the office of the man who had known the McGinnis family for many years. Slowly, Lambert explained that because of her friendship with Teddy, one of the grandest homes in New Orleans waited for her arrival. She would inherit a maid and caretaker as well. What he couldn't figure out was how this junkie would pay for all of the weekly maintenance on such a vast property. The entire sordid situation disgusted the attorney.

As she listened attentively to his words, a plan quickly formed in her mind. Susie may not have wealthy friends or high connections, but she had connections. She knew several dealers in the New Orleans area. What if they would agree to establish a "Hotel for Druggies" so to speak? They would offer cheap room and board to people who were too high to make it home and needed a place to crash. This place would be safe from the prying eyes of law enforcement. Here, they could squander days and not be concerned with discovery. It seemed very doable to her.

Joyfully, Susie signed the contracts as she smiled at the man who had just changed her life. Good ole Teddy had provided more than a good time for the woman; he now established her future.

Quietly, she laughed as she considered Carolyn who always hated her. Poor Carolyn, who always thought that Teddy loved her, had no idea of the contempt that Teddy and his friends held for the privileged woman. The McGinnis family were haughty and condescended to people like Susie. As she signed the final document, she laughed. Mr. Lambert looked at her with confusion.

"I thought that Teddy was a friend, maybe an old lover. You do understand that his death provided this gift for you. Surely, you must be sad at his horrific crash."

"Easy come, easy go, I guess. What I am aware of is this big house waiting for me. Where is my plane ticket?"

Lambert smiled. "The gravy train ends here, Susie. It is now up to you to provide funds for your future. Perhaps you should consider selling the house." Already, a plan existed. Susie appeared stoned most of the time, but she was street smart.

"May I use your phone?"

Lambert shook her hand as he escorted her to the front office where his clerk provided a telephone. After consulting a directory, Susie made one call.

"Hello, Frankie? Have I got a plan for you, a business arrangement in New Orleans should allow you to deal and make a little money on the side at *Susie's Hotel?*"

The young Frankie listened with fascination as she described her idea. Lambert's secretary felt repulsed by the entire conversation.

"People who use drugs are so disgusting," Laura commented to a fellow clerk who only nodded as she looked at the young woman on the telephone with repulsion.

Within a few hours, Susie strolled into a local Western Union office to pick up funds from her friend Frankie which would allow her to start her new enterprise. If only Teddy could see her now. Even better, what if the parents who kicked her out for her bad habits when she was sixteen could only witness her today? Maybe, Susie would look them up someday and offer them a few dollars. Again, she laughed uncontrollably at her new-found wealth. This day was August 23, 2005. Over the beautiful Bahamas, another enterprise was forming. This monster would destroy many people's futures. Worse than a druggie who schemed to live off others fortunes, this monster would create havoc of unparalleled consequence.

# TWENTY-ONE: THE MONSTER

August 23, 2005, was the day that a monster raised an ugly, destructive head. This giant formed quickly and began to move toward the Gulf of Mexico. Katrina was the largest and third strongest hurricane ever recorded to reach land in the United States. Poor **House** sat waiting for her new owners with no idea what was about to descend. There would be two hells moving toward the beautiful *Claire's House.* Susie's friend sent enough cash to her so that she no longer needed to travel Economy. Susie Smith sat luxuriantly in the seat of First Class on a Delta Boeing 737. Still dressed in the cheap dress which Mr. Lambert provided, she didn't notice the smell after wearing it for two days. *I am a wealthy woman now. All of you snobs* must *deal with the likes of me.* Her laughter seemed inappropriate to the flight attendant who served the first of many glasses of champagne to the unappreciative customer.

**House** sat shined and polished by her housekeeper. What sort of people would grace her halls? She longed to be loved again. So many had come and gone from her boundaries. None compared to Claire and Babe but maybe this new person would at least appreciate the exceptional beauty which surrounded the antebellum home.

Already, **House** decided that she did not like the name, Susie. The structure decided to hold judgment until this new person arrived.

Unbeknownst to **House**, the monster pulling into her drive was nothing like the monster quickly approaching. Traveling straight toward the beloved city of New Orleans was a four hundred mile long ravager of lives. Not only would she hit with a vicious assault, but the aftermath would prove catastrophic. It would result in over a hundred billion dollars in damages. Levees built for

Category 3 winds could not hold this force which would peak at a Category 5. The sustainable winds of over one hundred and seventy-five mph would demolish most of the structures which attempted to stand. Neighborhoods built below sea level would suffer unimaginable flooding and devastation. Unsuspecting levees built to hold Lake Pontchartrain and Lake Borgne would prove unreliable. The swamps and marshes to the East and to the West of these structures would help propel this monster. There would be storm surges as high as nine meters in some areas. Heavy waters would seep through the soil as they combined with profuse rain and wind. At the end of the storm, nearly eighty percent of New Orleans would suffer damage from water. The Coast Guard would rescue over thirty-four thousand residents. This horror would unite the city as never before. A neighbor helped his neighbor just to survive. Many people had nowhere to go. Mayor Ray Nagin would issue the first-ever mandatory evacuation of New Orleans. What were the one hundred twelve thousand innocent people of the over five hundred folks who did not have access to a car supposed to do? The city did the best that it could by offering the New Orleans Super Dome as an evacuation resource. Soon, they ran out of supplies as more and more victims arrived. Authorities accepted over fifteen thousand more refugees than they were equipped to care for before locking the doors and refusing entrance. Some tried to walk to Gretna over the Crescent City Connector bridge but were blocked access by officers with shotguns.

Especially devastated were low-lying places like St. Bernard Parish and the Ninth Ward. Eventually, they took on so much water that calls came from people in attics and those standing on rooftops. Early morning around 6 am on August 25, 2005, just as Susie meandered into her new life, Katrina began her assault on the Gulf Coast. She arrived with winds over one hundred forty-five miles per hour. At 8 am, the storm's eye passed over eastern New Orleans. For over a week, the terror flowed in the usually lively streets which were now deserted. Eight days later, residents were allowed to visit their home sites only to be evacuated the next day because of danger from polluted water standing in the streets. Thirty-three days after her arrival, the area still suffered from the influx of this monster of epic proportions. Not only was life destroyed, but the entire complexity of the state changed. Before the storm, the city's population mostly was black which was about sixty-seven percent with thirty percent of those living in poverty. Many died or were displaced to other areas. Nearly two thousand perished as over ninety-thousand square miles of the United States became decimated.

The rains began as the taxi moved slowly into the driveway of the beautiful antebellum mansion. Already, Fred, the driver decided to head home to check on his family. His passenger didn't care about storms. Her only thought was how much money she might make from her new venture.

## TWENTY-TWO: HELL

Early on a densely clouded day, the rains began in the early morning hours. Many had already evacuated to the Super Dome in downtown New Orleans. Little did they know that a hole would rip into the very structure meant for their protection. The remaining people had no idea how bad it was about to become.
**House** shook with rage at the straggly invaders of her space. From where had these horrible people come? Not only were they crude, but they were also inhospitable to many who knocked at the door begging for entrance.
It didn't matter, to these poor souls who banged on the massive doors for help, that the house was a fashion icon. The only concern for them was survival from the unrelenting rain.
Torrential rains continued to cascade from the skies. By 9 AM, low-lying areas were severely flooded. These folks had nowhere to go. **House** longed to

shake her doors open. Yes, she had always been aloof and snobbish in her mannerisms, but this was life or death. How dare these invaders show such inhospitable behavior to those who only were trying to survive?

Inside, Susie and twenty-two drug users huddled together. The power came and went as winds pushed everything from their path. Suddenly, gunshots filled the air. Confusion arose inside of the gleaming white structure. Sounds of people running and cries of horror outside echoed through the building. The merry group inside lighted every candle available. Calvin walked to the door. Laughing with glee, he returned to his confused group. They were enjoying lots of beer, weed, and heavier substances as they celebrated a Hurricane Party.

"That crazy moron, James, is shooting at the invaders. He is telling them that they have to find another place to crash because none of them have any money." Thoughtfully, he looked at Susie.

"Hey, man, should we let them come inside? I mean, where are they going to go from here? There isn't another place for miles. I don't even understand how they made it this far." He looked at his hostess with hope.

"Are you crazy? We ain't letting those maniacs inside. Maybe, there might be a psychopath. No, from now on, if anyone tries to enter, we have James shoot them."

The others looked at each other. While they may be a reckless and selfish group, they weren't killers. None of this was what Susie's friends had anticipated when they agreed to stay at *Susie's Hotel*.

Soon, James staggered back into the room. Shouting expletives of anger, he cocked his pistol.

"I've got a ton of ammunition. If these crazies keep coming, I'll fill them full of bullets." Like a crazed person, he laughed wickedly. The others looked at Susie who had also gotten a lot more than she planned.

Suddenly, James started singing, *Let's Get It On*! His voice was good. He sounded a little bit like Marvin Gay. The others danced or swayed to his silky rendition. Calvin shook his head at the entire situation with disdain. If he made it through this, he would be luckier by surviving than he had from the gang fights he endured on the streets of Baton Rouge, the state capital of Louisiana.

The group went back to the party. Noise from screams and cries outside the grand doors subsided.

Winds ravaged the area for about half the day and then began to relinquish their hold. The hurricane downgraded to a tropical depression, but nearly two thousand people perished, and over nine hundred folks were never located.

James, Calvin, Susie and the others spent several days in a stupor. Nothing mattered except the peace of knowing that they were safe and beyond the dangers of police detection.

**House** watched all of this in absolute panic. Even though she was built with the finest materials by the best builders; damage was significant. The roof sagged as a result of the pressure of so much water. Leaks appeared on the surface and allowed water into her massive attic. This deluge of water eventually poured through onto the floors. No one even tried to contain or stop the damage. If the owner, Susie, didn't care, why should they?

Miss Smith had never owned anything. She didn't have a clue about the importance of maintenance and avoiding damage. Instead, her laughter bounced off the walls which blistered and cracked. The beautiful walls which bore the finest paint in the world, Eurolux, even began to decay before the eyes of the ungrateful interlopers. Murano glass chandeliers loosened from their supports after over twenty years of peace.

Gorgeous, Macassar Ebony milled floors no longer shined but buckled due to massive water damage.

**House** watched her designer kitchen suffer. The huge Sub-Zero refrigerator smelled due to rotting meats from the power outage. Betty, the maid, had gone to great lengths to fill the larders with only the freshest products for the new owners.

**House's** Pyrolave kitchen counters stood bravely to the assault of wetness. It was hard to damage enameled lava. This durable volcanic stone covered with a glass coating came from volcanic craters in central France.

East Indian Rosewood cabinets could not withstand the barrage of water. Even the LeCournue range appeared damaged. **House** cried softly at her demise.

The finest bathroom fixtures in the world went unappreciated by this straggly group. The Acheo Cooper tub sat filled with water to flush the Toto

Neorest commodes. The most durable and expensive commodes in the world contained a built-in night light which had become inoperable during the power outage. The air freshener didn't work either nor did the motion detector which allowed the user to open the closed lid as they approached. This group urinated on the floors and ran the beautiful sinks with Waterworks fixtures to overrun. Such beautiful antique brass faucets were not appreciated but abused as the stragglers did damage to every structure in **House.**

The Hurricane Party lasted for over a week. Meanwhile, in New Orleans, people began to realize the depth of the destruction again when they were allowed to return home. None of this mattered to the irresponsibles inside of **House**. She shook with rage. So much wealth could have helped many people. The abuse leveled against **House,** by this small group, could not have been any worse. **House** had witnessed some

pretty awful things but nothing compared to the absolute willful disregard for life which could have found shelter in her arms. She longed to dispel these horrible people from her protection. Even the fire which consumed the structure during the time of Jake and Jasmine could not compare to the devastation she now suffered.
**House** felt broken.
The hurricane partiers left after some sibilance of normalcy returned. Another group arrived to fill the absence. A few years passed as Susie earned more and more money. Carefully, she saved and invested it.
*This abuse must stop and soon.*
**House** stood bravely holding these ungrateful in her strong arms. She did not have the answer as to how to dispel the savages. Months passed. The maid returned but quit due to the unbearable mess. Susie hired a group of cleaners. They wore masks as they attempted to remove the nastiness.

The new owner of **House** had made a small fortune from her ingenuity. Soon, even she tired of the damage done not just to her body but her beautiful home from her destructive lifestyle. As life began to settle, a new building firm was hired to replace the destruction from her *Hotel California* boys. Susie changed her name to Savannah which seemed much more refined to her. **House** watched all of this only grateful of finally reaching her once beguiling appearance.

## TWENTY-THREE: SUSIE OR SAVANNAH?

About two weeks after the workers left **House,** Susie woke early on a Saturday morning. The group never rose until late in the afternoon because they stayed up all night partying. The haggard woman walked to a mirror in her bathroom. Sadly, she studied the lines and creases that crisscrossed her potted face. As she stood at her mirror, out of the blue, she realized that this was her birthday. Never had she been considered beautiful. A bad complexion scarred her face back in her teen years. Since then, the drugs, booze, and cigarettes had created the appearance of a much older woman. Plagued by a hacking cough each morning, something deep inside her warned that she must change her ways or suffer from serious consequences.

Memories of a little girl with big, brown eyes caused tears to trickle from the same eyes which now were tired and lined. Life had not been easy for this one. Slowly, she walked to the door of the beautiful bath and locked it. Sunlight gleamed into the room in long slats through the plantation shutters. Who would have ever thought that this girl labeled a "loser" in high school could be the owner of such a magnificent mansion and acquire so much wealth? Yes, she had behaved in illegal actions, but there wasn't many choices available to her.

This damaged soul sat down slowly on the travertine floor. Carefully, Susie drew her legs into her thin body, the battered woman hung her head and cried so loudly that the sound alarmed even her. Quickly, Susie turned the overhead fan on to drown the wails of pain which assaulted the air.

The same memories, which assaulted her since early childhood, refused to be lay to rest. Maybe she had attained a better life, but the pain refused to leave the shackles of her mind. When would she finally discover the way to stop the unrelenting horror of what happened to her as a little child?

She was just a young girl when her drunken father stumbled into her bedroom late one night. The child trembled with fear. Able, her father, was never home. He lived with another woman and her children. When he visited her mom, Nancy, he was angry and mean. Usually, because Agnes, the other woman, had thrown him out. While he stayed for a night or two, he terrified his real wife and child. Now, he resorted to something so evil and vile that nausea resided in the stomach of an innocent. Her only crime was being the daughter of an immoral and heartless monster. Was her mother aware of the actions forced on such a young child? Susie shook with the realization that Nancy must have been aware. Today was the first time that her mind admitted this fact. The possibility of her mother knowing and not helping hurt as much as the physical abuse from her father. His assaults did not go without a fight. Susie had scratched and screamed to the top of her lungs for help. It never came. After repeated bouts of abuse, the screams stopped. Instead, she suffered alone. The girl's only recourse was to dream of a day when she may obtain vengeance on this man.

School days were hard. Susie had only old hand-me-downs. The other children bullied and abused her at school. There was no one or no place that provided comfort to a child so hurt and broken. The little girl refused to admit to anyone including herself, how damaged she had become from the abuse.

When she reached high school, a different group of young people welcomed her to the folds of "their group." They were the "losers" at school. Labeled as such because they also experienced horrors at home. Together, they experimented with any drugs that they could obtain. The pain, deep in their souls, was eventually filled with the thrill of ecstasy provided by prescription and street drugs. When money became depleted, the girls sold themselves for funds. The boys protected their charges on the street from jeers and abuse at school.

Susie cried for hours in front of her bathroom mirror inside beautiful **House**. Eventually, her eyes appeared red and swollen. Finally deciding, as she rose from her *pity party* that perhaps if she stopped the drug abuse, she might be able to stop the mental pain.

Carefully, the young woman studied her reflection. No, maybe she wasn't lovely, but she had seen much worse. The idea came like a load of bricks. Susie became Savannah in the shower. When she exited the room, her clean hair glistened with streaks of gray, but the smile which encompassed her face was that of a winner.

# TWENTY-FOUR: SAVANNAH'S HOUSE

Five days after Susie became Savannah, she felt like a different person. Savannah walked around the estate carefully studying her home. It was perfect again, since she expelled the druggies, due to months of work by an expert crew. There did not seem to be any other changes needed to upgrade it from a mess to a mansion again. The crews that she hired earlier had restored the beauty to **House** as in her earlier years. Savannah drove her convertible Lexus from **House** to New Orleans. She checked into the finest hotel and spent days shopping for a few refined objects for her beautiful home but mostly high-dollar expensive clothes for herself. The most elegant salon in town foiled her dry, brittle hair which soon glowed with highlighted blonde streaks.

The back of her car filled to the top with bags of lingerie and clothes fit for a Queen.

When she arrived at **House**, such joy filled her heart. Joy such as she had never experienced. Even **House** trembled as the current owner, who had never been up to **House's** expectations, entered with a new confidence and beauty. **House** could not believe the change.

"**House**, you should know that I'm now Savannah. I will never be simply Susie again." **House** liked the newly independent and confident person. She sure was easier to embrace. Even the latest perfume worn by her owner stirred **House's** admiration.

**House** didn't understand all of the phone calls which ensued. The owner spent many hours in deep conversations which reached all over the country?

*What was Savannah up to now?*

**House** felt a tinge of excitement. A new maintenance man took over the care of the shiny white structure. All of the signs crediting Claire and Clarissa to ownership soon lay in the trash. Bright, new signs proclaimed, *Welcome to the House of Savannah*. Why were so many signs needed? House couldn't figure it out.

A week later, deep in the night, as the lanterns around **House** glowed with the charms of gas flames, limousines arrived. Doors opened by chauffeurs. Elegant women sashayed from their carriages. Beauty once again filled the rooms of **House**. Such beauty that had left long ago. Again, laughter and music echoed into the dense night air. Flowers shed their luxuriant fragrance into the halls and rooms. The ambiance of pink, soft light calmed the spirits of the ladies assembled in the upstairs rooms of **House**.

Shortly, other cars arrived. Fancy sports cars with tops lowered for the drive from New Orleans to **House**. Taxis brought men paying hefty fairs from the airport. **House** trembled with excitement. This scene was fantastic! Happiness again reigned in a briefly dark place which once had shone with the brightest light. Except that, there was no light. The heavy drapes remained drawn even in the light of day. **House** glowed with beauty and ambiance, but no light could enter her.

Savannah welcomed the men with a crystal glass filled with their favorite drink. She flirted with each of them. Money graced her dainty palm which proudly displayed perfectly manicured nails. Her pitted face now shined with perfect skin. If she were not past forty, maybe she would have waited in one of the twenty bedrooms upstairs. Her role was much easier. All she needed was to be discreet, look beautiful, and take the money. Savannah smiled as she locked the door the next morning. An entire day waited for her to sleep and lounge by the pool. Tonight, the same scenario would repeat. Money flowed like the liquor in poor, unsuspecting **House**.

## TWENTY-FIVE: MADAME SAVANNAH

Savannah was now fifty-five years old. **House** glowed with years of constant loving care. Each day, fresh flowers were delivered by a professional florist. A golden harp sat in the foyer so that the busy, successful gentlemen felt ushered into **House** with a soft, festive greeting. However, this was no angel welcoming them to a sea of class, sophistication, booze, and sex. No indeed, the famous Madame, *Savannah of New Orleans,* opened the massive door with a sweet smile. She may look like an older, faded angel but she was not! This wily character amassed a fortune, not through kindness and charity, but a cut-throat approach to making her money. Sheer force resorted to blackmail and intimidation in advertising her wares and keeping reporters at bay.

The life of a Madame agreed with Savannah. She had never appeared so polished and smooth. No one would ever suspect that she recreated herself from a druggie vagrant right off the streets to a woman of renowned sophistication. Although you could not say that she gained respect in the higher circles, in her world, no one could compare with Madame Savannah!

**House** only knew that not a single homeowner stayed with her as long as the "Angel Savannah." Not only had Savannah taken wonderful care of her, but the relationship between the Madame and **House** was also warm and secure.

Each night, while the men and women met in darkened rooms, Savannah would sing as she softly rubbed the shiny walls. Her melodious voice agreed with the pinging of the golden harp strings. Lucy, the black musician who played the singing instrument, smiled as the Madame softly suggested the next tune. Together, they made beautiful music. **House** was proud of the owner who loved her and filled her passages with joy again.

Savannah now rose early unlike times in the past years. On one such morning, she walked to the full-length mirror in her bedroom. Carefully, removing her clothes and studying her aging body, the Madame cried. Although she had grown hardened by the blows of a trying and abusive life, tears flowed down her recent face lift.

Aging presented a particular challenge to this beautiful woman. Watching the quality, which she had desired all of her life, now fade caused grave concern for her. Sure, the Madame had never been considered beautiful, but because of a facelift and other surgeries, she now did possess the loveliness she always dreamed of achieving. After turning heads for only a short time, she felt forced to watch the fleeting asset fade more and more each day.

Slowly, she removed her clothing. Tears continued to fall. The only love she had ever actually known was from Teddy, but in the end, even he betrayed her when he married Carolyn. Why was she so unlovable? Clearly, the answer was apparent: who could love a Madame? At that moment, she decided that she possessed enough money to live well for the rest of her life. In fact, it would prove impossible to spend it all. Why should she continue shaming herself? When she visited New Orleans, she felt the glare from others. As she ate alone in the finest restaurants, patrons would point and whisper about her. Savannah developed a thick skin out of necessity. It was not the way that she desired to live by feeling inferior to others. What if she could find a nice man who might love her? Together, they would travel and enjoy her fortune. Trying to do this alone was impossible.

Carefully, she continued to remove her underwear. Yes, her body was older but still attractive. Someone could surely love her. Savannah never considered that she might find love for reasons other than beauty.

Now completely unclothed, gently, she lowered herself to the massive gold and red Persian rug which covered the floor. So many times, she played the mental tape of the abuse leveled against her when she was a child by the monster of a father. What right did anyone have to make another's life Hell? There would be justice in the next life, but what about now? If this poor creature could find love and respect now, wouldn't she experience retribution? Silently, she pondered this.

Her mind no longer broke with the pain she suffered as a young child at the hands of the person who should have protected and loved her. So many tears fell in the past that there were no tears left for that memory. Sometimes, she believed that she smelled soured gin breath breathing in her innocent face as his rough hands treated her as if she possessed no value. In her mind, his rude comments and grunts were not just an assault on her innocence, but her very being. Savannah detested him and what he represented: a sick, savage individual without a conscience. Never had he bothered to beg forgiveness.

Her father's hurtful ways were not the only battle that she endured. What about the time in seventh grade when a group of teenage girls bullied her for two years making her dread attending school? It was necessary for the young Susie to decide whether to suffer at their hands as she was forced to endure the taunts and insults from a group of spoiled, shallow girls or suffer at the hands of her father. She never missed a day of school for two full years to avoid the worst possible abuse, not from classmates but the man who may be waiting at her home. Even though the pain that they subjected felt difficult to bear, the torture from her father was worse.

The tape of those times began to run as she stretched out on the luxuriant carpet.

It seemed necessary for her to experience each major pain of her life right now. No matter how painful the tapes of childhood proved, Savannah was unable to stop the horrific images which slowly rolled in her head.

Already, she relived the trauma from her parents but now, she played the waiting tapes of mental abuse.

Copious tears cascaded from eyes which had seen way too much pain Why would anyone scratch old memories which remained safely filed in the mind bank under bad news? Still, even though she tried to think of **House** and happy thoughts, her mind refused to obey.

She was twelve years old on the first day of her seventh-grade year. Sadly, she pulled on the same old clothes from the past year on that early morning. They still fit although a little snugger than the previous year. Susie and her mother, Nancy, did not eat three meals each day. Susie enjoyed free breakfast and lunch at school. She had no idea what Nancy ate.

Nausea filled the young girl's stomach with a sourness on that day long ago. Slowly, she walked outside. Her mother slept until the afternoon. The day was overcast and hot. It was a long walk to the school, but she didn't mind. The peace and quiet greeted the girl after a summer mostly spent inside with the unrelenting television which her mother refused to turn off.

Things went well for Susie that first day. Several of her friends from elementary school shared the same class. The girl didn't have many friends, but just a few made it bearable. For some reason, six days after the new year began, she was called to the front of the class. Her teacher handed her a paper and told her to report to a different class. The girl had been pulled from this one. If she had parents who were involved in school affairs, this would never have occurred to the girl that no one seemed to love.

This news didn't affect her. What difference could it possibly create if she was forced to change classes? She wouldn't rock the boat. Things appeared to be going well for her. Susie Smith may experience acceptance at last! Quickly, she found the new class and entered with a smile.

When the final bell rang, Susie no longer laughed. The new class contained mostly people that she did not know. None of her friends existed there. Six of the new girls took an instant dislike to her. Although they didn't know her, they decided she wasn't worth knowing. Who wore old clothes? Her hair hung in her eyes. What was wrong with this loser? As the girl exited the red brick school building, she witnessed four of them laughingly enter a brand new Cadillac. These girls had someone to look out for them. This poor girl had no one.

"Who was that loser? She will be fun for us to push around. Apparently, no one

has ever seen her at 'The Club.'"
Everyone laughed.
"Are you kidding? Who are her parents? They would never let that group into our club."
More laughter erupted from the shiny car as they slammed the door and drove away. Susie stood on the curb. The words hurt. As the car slowly passed, one of the girls held up her middle finger as another lowered the back passenger window. "Freak" they shouted. Susie looked at the mother who drove the vehicle. She threw back her head and laughed. Once again, pain directed at her by an adult who should have known better.
Each day, those six girls created havoc on the other girls in the class. They made the others feel dirty and embarrassed as they continually called them *freaks* or *losers.*
No one ever confronted them. Maybe the *mean girls* were correct. Compared to the beautiful girls with expensive

clothes, those words did seem to apply to the poor students who didn't know that a club existed.

The day was Hell for everyone but the Fabulous Six. That was what the group called themselves. Susie went home each day and dreamed of being beautiful. She pretended that she was one of the Fab Six. Her dreams filled with scenarios of spending time after school with them. Thoughts allowed her to be just as beautiful and well-mannered as they. How did they know to hold eating utensils all the same? No one ever told her the correct way to dine or how to set a table. Susie had never heard of manners or etiquette. Her mom just said, "Be nice to everyone."

What happened to that suggestion? The *mean girls* weren't pleasant to anyone but each other. The boys in her class loved the *mean girls.* There was a group of attractive guys who had the same mindset as the six girls. Those kids picked on and berated the other boys who weren't fortunate enough to be wealthy. Susie felt sorry for some of the boys. At least, she and the girls could cry if things became too uncomfortable, not that they would ever let those meanies see them. Still, for the boys, it was worse.

Savannah realized the time wasted by reliving these hurtful moments in her life, but she just could not stop her mind. It seemed to control her. Since childhood, this walk during the most painful memories of her life refused to abate. For the rest of the day, those especially painful moments of her life flashed before her eyes. Maybe she was never aware of the depth of the pain neatly packaged in the recesses of her mind.

Savannah assumed the fetal position as she continued to relive moments of the past. A smile kissed her lips when she thought of high school. That was the happiest time of her entire existence. Attacks of anxiety no longer plagued her then as she waited at the bus stop. Instead, she gained acceptance with a small group of like-minded friends. Maybe they had not been accepted by the likes of jocks and cheerleaders, but they made sure that each other felt important in their tiny group of long-haired, hard rock inspired teenagers. The other ingredient which created a bond between the renegade group was drugs. Nothing too hard, but they all smoked weed and used prescription drugs. Eventually, as they neared graduation, the substances became harder to obtain. The girls became prostitutes to score the needed products while the guys protected them in the streets where they worked. Susie never understood the degree of which these friends used her until she was involved in an altercation one day. No one was available to protect her. Instead, they all ran away. Such disappointment seemed to be her lot in a sad hell-of-a-life. She faced imprisonment for dealing drugs and prostitution.

Her mother tired of her daughter's ways and inability to find work. Disgusted that Susie failed to graduate from high school and help with finances, Nancy threw her out of her home. Savannah hung her head in sadness. Where had her parents been in all of this? Later, where were the friends who promised to love and protect her? It seemed that everyone she loved and trusted only disappointed and betrayed her.

The discouraged woman rocked back and forth on the lavish carpet which covered the floor of her elegant bedroom. Suddenly, she looked around. "You have done all of this. See what you have accumulated? Why are you sad and discouraged? Maybe you aren't the 'salt of the earth,' but you've made your way on your own."

Her mind continued to hold her hostage as it paraded before her eyes many men. Savannah realized that she could not remember them all. So many times she thought that this would be the true love. Why did love escape her? Teddy came to mind. That was the one man who loved her. She was confident of his love. Still, he chose Carolyn over her. The inability to control this pain made her feel weak and defeated.

Deliberately, Savannah rose from the sea of moroseness which surrounded her. The late afternoon light now streamed into **House.**

*How shiny and white the walls gleamed!* Maybe the world considered her a failure of low moral values, but Savannah knew she had beaten the odds. Magnificence greeted her as she strolled into each room of **House.** Out of the blue, the small woman considered the fact that most of the grief and pain in her life resulted from bad choices of her making, notwithstanding the abuse of her father and mother. Now, she realized that in many ways, her mother was just as guilty as the father who abused her.

What was an innocent child to do? Of course, she was off-track in her life, but it wasn't too late. Hopefully, there would be many years ahead. It was imperative that if she expected to gain respect and acceptance, she must clean up her life.

For the first time in her existence, the woman thought of the unlimited opportunities which waited for her. Savannah walked to the phone and made only one call.

"It is over. I am shutting down my service. You take care of this. The code to the gate will no longer work for you. No one will be answering the door."

Then she phoned her travel agent.

"Book me on the most expensive cruise line. I want to sail to Europe. Take care of all arrangements. Only the finest accommodations should be made for me. I want to leave right now."

Excitement overcame the woman. Savannah always felt unimportant and inferior. Not now, she had made the most important decision of her life. Savannah Smith had turned over a new leaf. No more bad choices would define her. The abuse she suffered would make her stronger not hold her back. No more would she wallow in the unacceptable pain of her childhood.

Proudly, she pulled her slumping shoulders back as she packed for a trip which would spare no expense. The light which streamed into **House** now turned to a darkened twilight. Savannah opened the door for her driver. A new life awaited her.

## TWENTY-SIX: WHO IS THAT LADY?

Savannah only packed one bag. No need to overpack, it would be easy to shop for whatever she may require. Since she had no idea of her destination, why make it difficult? In no time, slowly, she strolled down the elegant staircase. Savannah watched herself in the ornate mirror hanging over the stairs. She procured the appearance of a well-educated, groomed lady of high means. In her heart, she realized that Susie Smith was a self-made woman of the streets. A voracious reader, the woman, would teach herself etiquette and manners. Over and over, she would practice the proper use of eating utensils. The image of the *mean girls* forced her never to repeat the feelings of inferiority that resulted from their polished manners.
Savannah was smart enough to know that there were cracks in her elegant demeanor. Many mannerisms and much knowledge waited for her discovery.

The lady longed to be knowledgeable about art, music, and the finer things in life. What about wines? How would she order in the best restaurants in Europe? Never again would she embarrass herself by the lack of knowledge which caused her to appear uneducated and unrefined. The answer was simple. At that moment, her mind soothed as she realized that this was the perfect time to eliminate the wrinkles. Instead of socializing on the crossing, she would sleep and read. The elegant dining room of the ship would allow her to practice her newfound skills of proper dining. Would the sommelier work with her and teach her all of the basics of Wine 101? She would gladly pay extra for that knowledge. There was a piano in the Champagne Bar. The pianist would surely teach her all about music and the most famous composers.

*What a wonderful way to meet others!*
During the coming days, she would read all about flowers, fashion, makeup, and

entertaining. Interior decorating remained unknown to this simple creature. That knowledge would help her decorate other homes which she may acquire. **House** was too perfect for her to consider changing it.

The driver arrived when she stepped off the last step. As George placed her bag in the trunk, she said a final goodbye to **House.** The *White House* felt something different from her owner. Suddenly, the constant sadness which surrounded Susie disappeared. Savannah emerged. Stronger, bolder, and more confident, she may not have all of the finesse she needed, but it would come. Perhaps this new-found feeling of boldness would wane but she would constantly battle to maintain it.

George drove Savannah to the waiting private plane which flew her to New York. The driver who waited there transported her instantly to the Carlyle Hotel. The staff greeted her as if she was famous. The man who escorted her to a room appeared to be the manager. His smile calmed the nervous condition which caused her hands to shake. Those old feelings of anxiety shook her confidence once again. Would she never be the bold, confident woman whom she desired? Did everyone replay tapes from their childhood? Now, she determined never to repeat the unrelenting mental nightmares of years long ago.

When the handsome manager opened the door to her room, Savannah's loud sigh caused him to smile. The room's opulence greeted the shaken woman. Quickly, she entered. Double windows welcomed the woman to New York. The walls seemed to glow with a pale pink ambiance. An extra large bed pulled her like a magnet to its perfect arms of softness. The sheets were ironed to perfection, and the whiteness of them comforted her with a feeling of home. There was a small table set as a dressing table facing one of the windows. Bright colors on the rug pulled all of the elements together. Savannah slightly staggered as she realized the late hour. The man smiled again before she was able to collect a tip for him from her purse. She had no change. No worries, tomorrow he would be paid double for his troubles. Instantly, she phoned her travel agent with an awareness that no one would answer at this time. It pleased her when she heard the soft, Southern accent greet her. People reacted differently when they dealt with great wealth!

"It is me, again. I'm indeed sorry for the late hour. This hotel is magnificent. How many days do I have here? Please say that I am allowed time in the city before leaving on my European surprise." Savannah had asked to be kept in the dark about the trip which waited. Each day, the agent would email instructions so that a sense of mystery surrounded this particular time.

"Savannah, I knew that you would love it in the city. I'm good at my job, right?"

Quickly, Savannah agreed.

"Well, you have three days in New York."

Savannah smiled with relief. Why had she not considered all that she could learn just by observing the most fashionable people on earth? It became apparent to her that the purpose of this trip was to reinvent herself. When she emerged from the metamorphosis which surrounded her as the cocoon of a butterfly, she would be a different person. Maybe she could even learn a new language from one of the places that she would visit. So many possibilities filled the woman with hope. Anxiety disappeared as she realized that it was up to her to be strong and stop the abusive cycle that prevailed in her life. The shower in the hotel room was divine. Hot water cascaded onto Ms. Smith with force. The large, thick towel wrapped her in peace. The draperies remained opened as she speedily climbed into the generous bed. Her eyes studied the outside with interest. Could it be that she, Savannah Smith, rested in one of the most famous hotels in the world? With her new found wealth, she could afford the best in the world as she traveled anywhere she desired. Peace flooded over her as the bright lights outside her window drew the attention of a man who enjoyed the same view from another floor in the same hotel.

## TWENTY-SEVEN: NEW YORK

Savannah opened her eyes suddenly. As she studied the opulent room, an awareness of a definite change in the way that she felt greeted her. This change felt wonderful! Never had she sparkled with the confidence which bordered on boldness.

A knock on her door caused surprise. There had been no correspondence with the front desk since she checked into the hotel. Ms. Smith grabbed the towel which remained at the foot of the bed from last night's shower. As she wrapped it around her, she strutted to the door. There stood a waiter with a small silver tray which was covered. He smiled. "Hello, Ms. Smith, I am Theodore. Your travel agent suggested that we welcome you each morning with a pot of our finest coffee and a French croissant with French butter. May I serve you? I am very sorry if I have disrupted the morning. We do not usually wake our visitors, but your agent insisted." He looked at her with an uncomfortable glance.

"You know what, this is perfect! I may have remained in bed all day, but who does that in New York? Please, serve me." Savannah opened the door widely for his admission.

Theodore sat down the tray and exited quickly without looking at her again. The naked woman with a towel was surprised until she realized that her backside was exposed. She laughed wickedly.

A plan for her time in the city formulated as she enjoyed excellent coffee. She had never eaten a French croissant or French butter. This pastry was better than anything that she knew. Without thinking, she gently hugged herself as she did when she needed comfort just like when she was a child. The woman did not hurry as excitement slowly built for the day ahead. When she finally dressed in a Channel navy slack suit with Spectator navy pumps, she softly closed the door as she exited her room.

*Wow, I'm used to doors which bang hard. This place thought of everything. I will make it a point always to stay here when I visit New York.* Again, she softly hugged herself for assurance. Maybe she was not as bold as she earlier thought.

"Good morning, Ms. Smith we hope that you enjoy your day."

Savannah staggered slightly. This man was not the clerk who checked her in last night. How did he know her name? The woman walked briskly outdoors. The sky was cerulean blue with not a cloud. A gentle wind blew her blond highlighted hair into eyes of brown which glowed with happiness and excitement.

Slowly, the woman meandered down 35th E 78th Street interested in everything that she encountered. Yes, she possessed great wealth but not class. Her mother told her a long time ago that

she would never, "Amount to anything. Class is not learned. You either have it, or you don't. My dear, we don't."
Those words rang in her ears.
"Maybe you didn't, but I will."
Loudly, the words echoed down the street. Those who passed looked at her with a smile. *Another crazy one*, they thought. Savannah didn't care. This city was New York, the greatest city on earth. New Yorkers were accustomed to seeing it all.
The woman, who dressed for success, continued walking until she reached 5th Avenue. When she crossed the street, she stopped. All of her life, she dreamed of standing right here. In front of the famous Tiffany's. Yes, the color was just as she imagined. How would these snobs react to her? Could they see that she was a phony? Maybe she dressed the part, but money could do that. Real class, they would recognize.
As she entered the prestigious store, she imagined for a moment that everyone

stared at her. It was impossible to move. Would they yell for her to leave? As hard as she tried, her feet refused to cooperate. The faces of the *mean girls* looked at her. Finally, Savannah timidly walked to one of the sparkling counters. It revealed many gold watches. She did not own one. Carefully, her eyes roamed the exhibit. Within twenty minutes, she purchased just the watch that the clerk recommended. The gold Rolex watch reflected light as the clerk snapped it onto her small arm. Never, had Savannah seen such a gorgeous timepiece.

"Ms. Thomas, you don't seem very busy right now. Would you mind teaching me about jewelry?"

The older woman seemed confused. "Dear, I'm not sure what you mean. You simply buy what you like. Money doesn't appear to be a problem for you." With interest, the two women looked at each other.

"No, it is not money that I lack; it is knowledge. Some people may say that I lack class. When I was a child, many people from my hometown referred to my family as 'trailer trash.'"

Now, she had the clerk's attention.

"Yes, I understand. You see, I was my husband's secretary. Hubert was a wealthy man. His family and friends said that he 'Married beneath himself.' I understand. You have come to the right place. I will teach you all that I know, but I may have to wait on other customers as they enter. While I do, please feel free to look around. When you leave, you will understand the art of 'fine jewelry.'"

Carefully, Savannah produced a small roll of bills to the unsuspecting woman. Ms. Thomas smiled.

"Don't even think of it. Consider this a gift from one piece of trash to another."

Both women laughed uncontrollably. Savannah put the bills back into her purse. So much for the myth of the

*Insensitive New Yorkers,* Savannah thought. *Ms. Thomas's action was one of the kindest acts that I have ever encountered.*

The day passed quickly as the two visited each counter. When she finally left the store, Savannah knew without a doubt that she could recognize most costume pieces from real ones. All of the major brands, she now knew. This lesson was the most fun class in which she had ever participated.

After she stepped outside, she noticed a restaurant. Breakfast this morning was light. *The Modern* enticed her entrance. It was a hip place with an unusual fare. Once the hungry patron was seated, she noticed that many others dined alone. The food was fresh and exciting. Although the portions seemed small, she was not faced with a menu of massive, tempting choices. It was enlightening. New York fascinated Savannah. Aware that she had two more days in this bustling place pleased her.

Next, Ms. Smith visited the Museum of Modern Art. Hours slowly ticked forward. Quietly, she talked with other patrons as well as members of the staff. Most people were happy to explain what they saw as they studied the art. Savannah soaked up knowledge of famous artists. So quickly, time leaped forward. The others came and went, but this woman stood alone.

At last, her stomach announced more food was needed, so she began to walk back to the Carlyle. When she entered her new home, the ambiance greeted her with peace. A new desk clerk welcomed her back. How did these people know her? Exhaustion ebbed over the lady. Alone, she entered the legendary bar. Would she see anyone famous? It was cocktail hour. Savannah lumbered toward a place in the corner. Quietly, she observed as she enjoyed a Gin Martini. Laughter erupted from across the room. Each time she heard boisterous laughter, she thought of the *mean girls*. These were no *mean girls*. A group of young men huddled together talking. Most likely, they were Wall Street executives. They didn't even look at her. One of the men was most extraordinary looking. He stood taller than the others, and he dressed in an expensive suit; his dark hair gleamed pulled back from his face. It glistened with vitality. His dark eyes shined with intelligence and mischievousness. If only she could meet him. Sadly, she hung her head. Someone like him would never be interested in the likes of Savannah Smith. Slowly, she finished her drink and walked into the dining room.

It was too early for most people but not her. She tired of being social. As she dined in the back of the room, she read a book that she carried in her purse. The latest novel prevented her from feeling lonely. In fact, she relished the time by herself. Loneliness was nothing that she feared. No, it was others with selfish motives that frightened her.

Laughter caused her to look up. The same group of men from the bar entered. Their loudness seemed inappropriate in this haven of peace. Quickly, Savannah completed her meal. The group sat by the door. As she left, her eyes inadvertently looked directly into the brown eyes of the most handsome man. Fire burned in her soul as their eyes met. She felt herself blush violently. She tripped slightly over her own feet. He must think her a fool. Instead, the look which he gave her showed interest. A small nod from him frightened her. Quickly, she almost ran from the room. Breathing became difficult as she realized that this man seemed interested in her. Her, Savannah Smith, she must be wrong.

## TWENTY-EIGHT: THE BOOKSTORE

Savannah rushed back to the safety of her enchanting room. Immediately, she entered the rush of hot water in the shower. As she stood under the hot stream of liquid heat, she thought about all of the men in her life. No one ever really loved her. Teddy was the biggest disappointment because she thought that he was the one who truly did.

She laughed loudly at such a silly notion that someone like that handsome man that she saw downstairs could be interested in the likes of a street druggie, Madame, who was never loved. These thoughts were ridiculous.

Her mind refused to stop thinking about the dark-haired man with eyes the color of coal. His eyes weren't brown; they appeared black with a twinkle which touched her soul. Unable to control the thoughts which assaulted her mind, she dreamed that they walked together in a mystic place. This scene was a place where she had never visited. Vineyards covered the uneven terrain. She could smell the sweet fragrance of large, purple grapes. Then she realized it was her shampoo that aromatized the room. Again, she laughed. What a silly woman!

Savannah snuggled into her feather bed once again naked after the shower. The bedding was rich; the ability to feel the texture of such fine linens created a sense of comfort and luxury. **House** came to her mind. As if she thought of a friend, instantly she relaxed. The room felt cold, so she pulled the plump duvet up to her chin and squeezed down into the luxury.

"Dear **House,** you have brought me so much joy. I miss you and dream about you. No matter how perfect or enticing any other place may be, you hold the keys to my heart. Surely, you know this."

The distant image of **House** standing steady as she waited for the return of her owner caused a tinge of homesickness. **House** was her only friend.

All through the night, the constant thought of the man with black hair and eyes controlled her dreams. Over and over they walked the magical place of blue skies and vineyards. The terrain was flat with unlimited lavender. Rosemary and juniper grew in abundance as did beds of giant, happy sunflowers. The couple stood by an ancient olive tree. The stranger held her hands. Dreamily, she gazed into eyes darker than the center of the golden flowers which surrounded them. Lovingly, he explained the history of that gnarled, old tree. His voice lightly spoke. His speech was different. Savannah understood, he was French. Quickly, she sat up in bed. Yes, that was the reason that she ran. The group of men were French. When he looked at her, the others turned toward her, their interest in her frightened her because she could not understand what they said.

Had they made light of her? Scarred by the experiences of her past with the *mean girls* and the men who used her, any time that she felt scrutinized, it caused her to run.

*I hope that I never encounter him again. It is enough for me to dream of him.*
Sleep descended, but it was a tumultuous night. His face burned into her mind. Morning came much too quickly. Sleepiness prevented her from answering the knock on her door quickly. She moved as if in a trance. Even though she thought last night that she never wanted to see him again, her desire was that she would. His memory would haunt her until the end of her life. Theodore obviously had a better night than she. Cheerfully, he entered with his small tray. After setting the small tray on her bedside table, he pulled the drapes apart. Savannah smiled as she sighed. At least she had covered her backside this morning. He did not seem frightened by her. The thought of the waiter telling the

others of the crazy, old woman who answered her door half-naked stimulated her. The tired, drained, earlier feeling fled. Only new interest piqued her mind. Yesterday, a plan formulated. Today, she knew exactly where she would enjoy her time.

Today was Friday, her last day in New York. This day was when her travel agent would phone with further details for her trip. Again, the image of the stranger with black eyes came to mind. Her hand automatically curled around emptiness, but it seemed that she felt his smooth hand inside her grip. Eyes of brown looked into black pools of hot coal. Her hand outlined the shape of his face. The color of his skin appeared deeply tanned. He did not seem to work outside in the heat, the aristocracy of his background would prevent his doing so. Savannah pulled a soft blue dress, the color of the sky, over her head. The luscious fabric made her scrunch her shoulders together to emphasize the feeling. Her favorite pair of matching flats agreed with the casual wear that she chose for this day. What did it matter? No one knew her; there was no reason to impress the clerks. They did not care. With her key in her right hand and her cream purse in the other, she waved "goodbye" to the room. This action was what she always did whenever she left **House.** A quick wave goodbye as if **House** could see her. The temperature in the hall of the hotel felt colder than that of her room which was icy. She wished that she had brought a sweater. Her plan would be ruined if she was faced with a frigid temperature all day. The project from yesterday ran through her mind again. Yes, this was the perfect way to enjoy her last day in the city. Hours inside this bastion of knowledge was just what she needed.

"**House**, are you okay? I miss you."
Her words echoed down the empty hall. The lobby was quiet. The desk clerk, the

same as yesterday, waved to her. The temperature in the pleasant entrance was perfect. Savannah couldn't help herself, slowly, she approached the dining room. Most of the breakfast crowd had already left for the day's activities. The woman had not meant to spend excessive time in her room, but thoughts of the handsome stranger and dear **House** had prolonged her stay there.

Shyly, she looked into the dining room. The table where he dined yesterday was empty. Sadness created a small frown.

"I believe that I know who you are hoping to see."

An attractive, young woman with long brown hair and shiny brown eyes smiled at her.

"Oh, no, I'm not looking for anyone. I'm a stranger alone in the city. I leave tomorrow on a long trip to a place that I have no idea the location. No one knows me, and I certainly know no one." She smiled back.

Savannah knew that she rambled and must sound foolish.

"Well, every woman who saw him yesterday is looking for him. You must be the only one who isn't interested. Did he not try to contact you? He asked the front desk about you, of course, they could give no information concerning you or any of our guests. I told the other gals to forget him. I figured that the two of you would show up together for breakfast today. He just left. I think that he was going home. He's French you know." Gently, she touched Savannah's hand, smiled, and was gone.

Staggering against the wall, the woman in the blue dress heard the rush of blood in her ears. Her dream, she had suspected that it was a location in France where they walked in fields of lavender. He was indeed French. The wild ideas were not so out of kilter. Did he actually inquire about her? For the rest of her life, she would remember this feeling of validation. Someone so impressive, who the other women swooned over, had chosen to ask about her.

Savannah pulled her shoulders back and glided into the lobby. Now, she could let the handsome stranger go for he was definitely gone from her life when he returned to France. No matter, she could now relax and enjoy her last day in the city. The doorman nodded at her.

"Taxi, Madame?"

"What, on a day such as this? No, thanks."

Another gorgeous day greeted her.

It truly was one of those New York days with nary a cloud. The sky was Carolina-blue with a gentle wind from the north-side. Her eyes studied each detail of her surroundings. Her life seemed drastically changed from the Louisiana Madame. No longer did she judge herself by her career. Instead, a new person inhabited the body of Savannah, the Madame. This new individual was Savannah, the beauty, the person of interest, and worth.

Quickly, she passed an expensive shoe store, a pair of Christian Louboutin black pumps pulled her inside as if a magnet.

"Madame, may I be of assistance?"

The older woman had an attitude. At one time, Savannah the Madame would have politely excused herself. Confrontations were avoided at all costs. The new Savannah was tired of such silly behavior.

"Well, since you are a sales clerk, and I am a customer, yes, you may help me. May I ask for a glass of water?"

The clerk studied her with new interest. She smiled.

"Yes, of course, Madame, only the best."

She continued to stand in the same spot as did Savannah. Finally, Savannah sat down. To her surprise, another clerk appeared with a bottle of chilled spring water.

"Now, what may I bring you?"

Savannah felt new-found respect from the employee who apparently loved to make customers squirm.

*You will never force me to feel uncomfortable again. I am as good as you. I am equal to the mean girls.*

Soon Savannah exited the over-priced store with a colorful bag which carried her beautiful new shoes. Tonight, she would wear them to dinner. The happy woman continued to walk down the street full of newly found confidence.

**House,** *if* you *could only see me now.* You *won't believe all of the stories that I can share with* you *on my return. Now where is that bookstore that I saw yesterday?*

She noticed the impressive granite entrance. Savannah walked inside. The store impressed everyone who entered. *What a safe, wonderfully enlightening way to spend the day as I learn more about how to behave in correct ways.* Carefully, she browsed shelves lined with English and French books. Quickly, she collected so many that she returned to the desk with her treasures.

"I'm taking a long trip. My destination is unknown; I'm waiting for my travel agent to phone me." She lowered her head.

People who rambled were a bother to Savannah. The clerk only smiled. When her cell phone instantly began to ring, the clerk appeared distressed.

"Perhaps, you might go inside that space over there to conduct your business with 'your travel agent.'"

No matter to the customer, she refused to be upset by senseless words of herself or others. Nonchalantly, she strolled to the designated area.

Laughter softly filled the small space. It was indeed her travel agent with the next part of her trip. Savannah listened carefully. She was breathless with excitement.

"Ms. Smith? I can barely hear you. Are you all right?" Ms. Smith smiled.

"Yes, I'm fine. You are driving me insane. I could hardly sleep last night with excitement. Where is my destination? Tell me it is somewhere divine. Maybe the countryside of France?"

The image of herself walking with the handsome man surfaced again. When would *he* leave her thoughts? She tired of being held ransom by him.

"It is indeed wonderful. In fact, it is the best. You, my dearest, are on your way to Portofino, Italy. Although it is not France, you will not be that far away from the French border. The beauty is that you can enjoy this place as well as being close enough to France. You should have told me that you wanted to visit the French side. Remember, you're the one who asked me 'to surprise you.' Do you prefer that I reschedule everything to France? You will not be disappointed by the Italian location."

The agent waited with a hefty sigh.

Before Savannah could respond, the travel agent continued.
"I have rented the most exquisite villa for you. It is incredible! My family and I enjoyed it last year. The house may be a little large for you but what the heck! You only live on this earth once."
Savannah realized "what the heck" meant *It will cost a small fortune.* She hesitated. Then, thoughts of all of the abuse during her life and the hardships she faced caused her to react. Her reaction was just what the other party hoped.
"No, don't you dare reschedule. It will be fun driving over the border. What a nice way to compare Provence to Tuscany; maybe next year, Provence will be the destination. Who knows? What the heck?" Savannah laughed loudly as did the clerk. Again *his* image surfaced. Could he live in Provence? "Miss, please, don't forget to be quieter." The sales clerk sweetly smiled as she stepped into *the space.*

*Yes, everyone is indeed sweet because I'm paying these people a nice chunk of money!*

"Now, here are your flight instructions. I have also faxed them to the Carlyle. The desk clerk will have them when you return. There are photos of the villa. It is a beauty. Of course, you are near the beach. A car comes with the property. Call me if you have questions. Okay, bye-bye." The phone went quiet as her conversation with the travel agent ended.

*Bye-bye? Instructions are at the hotel?* The old nervous jitters descended on the small woman. She found it difficult to swallow. What was she doing? An incredible home waited for her in Louisiana. Had she made a mistake taking such a long trip alone?

**House,** *what have I done?*

Savannah found an empty chair by the window and sat to read her latest book about Tuscany. Immediately, her spirits soared. What a destination! She couldn't wait for tomorrow to arrive. No, she had not made a mistake doing this. **House** would not recognize her when she finally returned.

## TWENTY-NINE: **HOUSE** AGES

**House** sat alone and empty except for the cleaning lady who arrived each day. The employees did not have the same effect on **House** as did her owners. **House** could not identify with those people. It seemed that as she aged, the connection to individuals had faded. The only connection that she now possessed was to Savannah. Happily, with great love, **House** remembered Claire and Babe as well as the entire Gautier family. Back then, it was possible for her to feel the emotions of Nanny as well as members of the Hinckley family. Clarissa's feelings were palpable to the structure. Now, she could only experience the being of Savannah.
It was true. **House** had proudly stood now for almost a century. Great amounts of money testified to the love that so many families felt for this unusual home. No expense had gone unpaid to maintain the opulence of **House.**

**House** trembled slightly. She now felt her age just as an elegant lady whose advanced years resulted in a slower gait and vulnerability.

It pleased the structure to remember all of the past owners. Many of them died in her arms except for the most beloved. The Gautier family had perished in a plane crash. She had not been available to experience their demise. That fact resulted in great pain for **House**. After all, this was *Claire's House*. Even though many people cared for her, especially Steven and Clarissa, no one could compare to Claire.

Just as an aged person has a mind which roams and becomes incoherent, **House** felt the effects of time. Sweet memories turned as yellowed pages from the past. Faces, long ago buried, surfaced again. She felt the Gautier children run down her polished halls. When they stroked her new, shiny white walls, **House** thought that she would never experience anything so special. Thoughts of Claire and Christophe sharing private moments in the master bedroom upstairs caused **House** to smile.

The thoughts slowly turned as the next owners walked across her threshold. Poor Lorraine, she had not meant any harm. Now, **House** wished that she may have been kinder to Mrs. Hinckley. Maybe her voice squeaked causing **House** to shudder, but today, **House's** reaction would be more tolerant.

Steven and Clarissa had never created any unpleasant feelings for the massive structure. They loved her. Sweet, lovely Clarissa created almost as much joy as Claire to the sweeping abode. Thoughts of those two still resulted in sadness for her.

Jake and Jasmine, maybe they were the saddest. Such beautiful people should have found joy in her outstretched arms. Not the horrible demise which shocked everyone. If only **House** could have understood the depth of the damages done to the soul of the great warrior.

Maybe, she could have protected Jasmine to a higher degree. Thoughts of those two always resulted in deep sadness for **House**.

Carolyn and Teddy never entered **House** as a couple. They crashed before **House** could know them. Still, the grand mansion did not like Carolyn. It was better that they never opened her gates. The vibrations from that woman were confusing. Although Carolyn could love others, she was selfish and mean-spirited. **House** could sense that so quickly.

Another sad pair was Bill and Mandy. How could he drop Mandy so quickly? Louise never cared for anyone but Louise. Mandy developed into a work of beauty before the eyes of **House**. When Bill betrayed her, **House** experienced such feelings of deception. Through the long years that she stood gracefully holding those who entered her gates, the Bivens story was the most shocking moment. Mandy trusted him. Louise hated him, but he chose the lesser of the two women. Did money decide the fates? **House** still struggled with that one.

Finally, Susie Smith sauntered inside the *White House.* Although she had been given many names, *Claire's House* remained **House's** favorite. Or was it? Lately, she felt such strong bonds to Susie Smith. When Susie became Savannah, **House** observed a metamorphosis, unlike anything which she had ever witnessed. No other person who lived in her ever craved acceptance like Susie. When she skillfully recreated herself, *Claire's House* became a little bit of *Savannah's House.* Even though the sign *Claire's House* once graced her doors, **House** now thought of herself as *Savannah's House.*

Twilight descended on the bayou of Louisiana where the high structure stood. Orange and golden streaks outlined the lake beside of the home to Savannah Smith. A gentle southern

breeze carried the night sounds of frogs and katydids. Pleasant smells of jasmine and honeysuckle sweetly perfumed the air which now turned black.
Estelle, the maid, stroked the walls of **House** with love. This lady had cared for many families and homes, but no one treated her as kindly and with the respect which Ms. Savannah showed her. That sweet woman loved this place. They almost seemed tied as blood. Estelle closed the massive door and locked it carefully. The responsibility of maintaining such expensive properties impressed the caretaker. She took her assignments seriously. When Ms. Savannah decided that she was no longer in need of her services, Estelle had already decided to retire. Years of hard work caused many aches and pains to torture the older woman's sleep.
The long drive to her tiny home inside another bayou area was dangerous due to diminished eyesight. She never felt bothered when she left the big house and

arrived at her simple cottage. That little cottage was hers. She had no illusions of being able to care for more than she owned. That was plenty enough for the woman who once lived with twelve siblings in a home much smaller than hers today.

**House** watched Estelle slowly walk to her old car and blink the lights *Goodbye*. The older woman did this each evening. The kindness which the caretaker showed **House** pleased *Savannah's House*. She finally voiced her feelings. Maybe she was named *Claire's House* but lately, something amazing had occurred, in her being, **House** knew that she had become *Savannah's House*. She smiled.

## THIRTY: THE ITALIAN RIVIERA

Savannah snuggled into her First-Class seat. She enjoyed a glass of champagne. The passenger held her breath as the British Airways flight climbed to cruising altitude. Silently, her prayer of thanks was raised.

This non-stop flight would transport her to Milan. From Milan, she would catch a smaller plane to Genoa. It would then be necessary to take a water taxi to Portofino. Savannah felt thankful that she only packed one bag. It just wasn't worth the effort of transporting a large amount of luggage.

Long, lazy days would not require many clothes. There would be plenty of stores to purchase what she may need.

Images of wearing only a beach cover-up most days made her smile. All of the books, which she bought before leaving New York, would be hard enough to carry. With that thought, she picked up the book beside her and began to read.

The flight would last all night plus the other flight in Milan to the water taxi. Tomorrow would be a long day. Never, would sleep come at such a stressful time because she feared flying. Savannah hugged the pajamas that she would soon wear. The seat would become a bed.

*What a way to travel!*

Her nerves were a little jittery, but she hoped a glass or two of champagne would soothe her.

Hours flew past as travelers around her walked past to change their attire. Lights were dimmed all over the plane as weary travelers found solace in the waiting bed. Still, Savannah read her book about art. Ever since she was a small child, thoughts of learning to paint filled her head. Not a great painter, she only wanted the ability to mix colors and understand basic procedures. These next few months would be her time to stop being afraid of failure and try to accomplish dreams.

After her attempt at art, she planned to learn everything possible about classical music and opera. She smiled as she imaged her mother's rude comments about her.

*Well, just look at you, Susie Smith. You are trying to be high-class, but you will never be anything but 'plain Susie,' so get used to it!*

Savannah hung her head. When would the scars of childhood finally be laid to rest? She often felt ridiculous reliving events of so long ago. The brave people, who were soldiers that volunteered for long, hot, dangerous years protecting their country, how did they not become angry and disappointed at the cavalier attitude from the people whom they risked their lives to protect? Soldiers had the right to feel emotional pain but not Susie Smith. Who gave her the right to luxuriate in the ridiculous pain of childhood? Surely, everyone had scars from that period of their life.

The flight attendant stopped by her seat.

"Miss, it is very late. Don't you want to prepare for bed now? I'll turn your seat into a bed while you change. You can continue to read later when you are settled if you want."

The traveler was now weary and longed for sleep, but Savannah hesitated to miss a moment of this journey. Just the same, she carried her pajamas to the restroom and prepared for bed. The airlines even provided a small toothbrush and paste for convenience. Suddenly, tiredness overcame her to such a degree that she staggered back to her bed.

"Please forgive me for staggering. I don't think that I had that much champagne?"

The attractive lady only smiled and covered her charge gently. Thoughts of childhood assailed Savannah once again. She could not remember anyone ever helping her to bed. What a comforting feeling of a soft touch even if it was from a stranger. Her eyes closed.

*I'll just close my eyes for a short time.*

When the noise of other travelers around her filled the cabin, she sat up. Bright light streaked in nearby windows. Had she slept the entire night without interruptions? The young woman yawned lazily and sat up. Quickly, she hurried to the restroom expecting a line. There wasn't anyone waiting. Seamlessly, she prepared for the day. She felt great!

*I can get used to this life.*

She automatically hugged herself as was her habit. The other passengers smiled and appeared happy.

When she flew from Genoa to Milan, it became difficult to focus. The Milan airport was a blur. Her mind felt confused, and her thoughts were jumbled although the flight was uneventful. She seemed to do all of the right things but fear descended once again. That old companion was as old as she.

*When would she finally arrive?*

Maybe she should have stressed that she wanted a simpler destination. All of this uncertainty felt exhausting.

Finally, the plane landed in Genoa, and she walked outside into the Italian weather. The indescribable heat hit her in the face! She was accustomed to heat and humidity, but not to this degree. This was a different sort of heat. Savannah staggered as she carried her bags of books and one piece of luggage. Maybe she should not have brought anything but herself?

How hard was it going to be trying to find a water taxi and where was she supposed to go? At that moment, she noticed a large tree which provided a small amount of shade. Rushing with all of her supplies was impossible, but she tried. As she did, she hit other people, but everyone was in the same condition as they searched for their next mode of travel.

While she sat under the tree, she noticed a shiny water taxi waiting for someone.

A young man held a small placard. It was impossible to read. Loudly, she sighed. If she struggled to carry all of her things and that was not her ride, it would be too much exhaustion in this heat. Still, it would not be wise to leave the things alone under the tree.

She waved at the young man. To her amazement, he walked toward her with the small sign. Her name displayed in black letters. Graciously, he assisted her as he carried everything to the taxi.

"My lady told me to look for the prettiest woman." He smiled brightly at her.

Probably a lie but it sounded nice.

*Conditions just improved.*

An earlier fear had been that the taxi would not be here, and she would be forced to wait for hours.

The taxi glided over the water as they soared toward Portofino. The blue sky displayed fluffy white clouds. The wind in her face felt divine while salty sea aromas caressed her tired face. Her

dress, now saturated in perspiration, began to dry in the wind.
Savannah pulled a foldable hat from her bag. That hat coupled with large sunglasses should protect her face until they arrived in Portofino.
Now the boat increased speed. As they left some of the clutter behind, Savannah breathed in the delightful smell of the seaside. Soon, they approached the town, her breath caught in her chest. Many sailboats anchored all around her. *This area must be one of the most beautiful places on earth!*
Without meaning to do so, the image of the handsome Frenchman filled her mind. She pretended that he sat beside her as they zoomed toward their seaside, summer home. A small giggle escaped her when she felt his hand gently hold hers. The boatman smiled back at her.
"Madame, I hope that you don't mind my saying this, but the home that you rented is one of the prettiest in this whole resort. If you should need

anything, I will give you my card. Please feel free to call."

He produced a toothy smile displaying the whitest teeth she had ever seen. Suddenly, he turned the boat sharply. "We have arrived, Madame."

Savannah had no idea what that meant or what she was supposed to do. Sitting in the same spot, she observed the young man carry all of her things onto the dock. He held out his hand. She accepted it as he pulled her out of the vessel and onto the boardwalk. He gave her a business card, and he was gone. Alone, on the dock, the young woman watched as everyone around her seemed to know what they were doing and where they were going. It occurred to her that she knew no one and could not speak the Italian language. She should have known fear, but she did not. The entire scene was mesmerizing. People scurried all around as she sat on her suitcase and waited for, what?

As she sat alone, observing the orderly movement of her new townspeople, a feeling of deep contentment overcame her. Once again, she realized that she possessed enough money that there would be few problems for her the rest of her life. Worst case scenario, she would have to find a hotel, but there appeared to be many, so that should not be a problem.

Fearlessly, she sat there on the dock alone and waited.

*What a gorgeous place!*

**House** came to her mind. A smile kissed her lips as always when she remembered her love.

The bluest water reflected the sun as she watched the large clouds slowly move over her head. The large shadows, created by the fluffy clouds, moved slowly over the ground. She studied the darkness which they created on the water. At times, the waters seemed green but then changed to a cobalt blue.

The buildings surrounding the coastal waters were most impressive. Bright colors pulled her eyes with reds and golds. So, this was the Italian Riviera? It was more than she had ever dreamed. The town was an ancient city which sat on a natural harbor. Generations of families lived and died here. Would they embrace this American stranger? She could only hope.

Savannah breathed the salty, hot air. Here, it was not nearly as hot as back at the airport. The breeze off the bay cooled and soothed her.

A small man approached. He was very tanned and wore a white shirt with a straw hat. Dark glasses protected his eyes from the sweltering light.

"Ms. Smith? I am sorry. It seems that I got the time wrong. Usually, I'm waiting for my residents. Please, please forgive me." He hung his head.

"There is no need to apologize. I have enjoyed observing my hometown for the next three months. It is not so different from any port town. Right?"

Her smile was quick and sincere. Gustus readily returned it as he picked up all of her things with one sweeping gesture. He carried it effortlessly even though he was a small man. Savannah liked him. The driver led the way to a bright red Fiat Spider. The top was down. Gustus threw everything into the back seat. Savannah was glad that there were no precious items. She strapped on her seat belt. Together, she and Gustus headed up a steep hill.

"Welcome to the Italian Riviera, Madame. You will love Portofino!"

"I already do!" She returned his big smile

# THIRTY-ONE: THE OTHER HOUSE

Savannah was terribly disappointed that the villa wasn't located on the beach. It was her fault; she realized that, but she assumed the travel agent would know. She sighed loudly.
*Never assume. It's my fault.*
Gustus smiled broadly at the woman whose mind continued to wander.
*I can't wait to swim nude in the heavenly waters.*
*No need for expensive clothes, I'll dress mainly in beach cover-ups. Maybe I'm not located directly on the beach, but I'll go there each day!*
"Right now, you are disappointed that you are not located directly on the beach. Right?" His English was broken but charming.
"You see, all of our guests think the same thing. I can guarantee you that when you leave us, it will break your heart. Your villa is one wing of a very old, historic home. There are

breathtaking verandas and terraces to woo you. A surprise waits for you which will break the disappointment of not being directly on the beach. We realize that you pictured yourself swimming nude in the pristine waters and wearing only a beach cover-up most times." Again, the broad smile melted her disappointment.

"Gustus, how did you know this? Are you a mind reader as well as an excellent driver?"

Savannah lied. He was Italian. They are notoriously terrible drivers by English standards.

"No-no, I know because every beautiful American woman who comes here alone is searching for the same thing. A safe residence, a gorgeous tan, and an Italian boyfriend are all prerequisites."

He touched her left leg. It wasn't a threatening motion, but it still created discomfort. Savannah moved his hand. Then immediately grabbed the armrest.

Her knuckles were blue from holding it tightly. The driver was a horrible one.
"Gustus, you just blew your record as a mind reader. You are obviously right on the first one, but I easily become freckled by the sun so no tan. An Italian boyfriend is not on my agenda either, maybe a French one."
This answer caused Gustus to rant against the French.
"We, Italians, are great lovers. The French are chefs and decorators."
They both laughed gaily.
The drive to the villa was quick. As Savannah left the Fiat and entered the house, she smiled. Already, she changed her mind. This location was perfect. Here, she was off the beaten path and away from the noise down at the beach. Gustus was correct; the villa was breathtaking.
"Did the agent tell you that this beautiful car and driver come with the house? That's-a-right. For the price of this breathtaking villa, you get the car, if you

want to drive, or me, if you don't. I wear many hats around here. You see, Gustus is multi-talented. My mastery of the garden is legendary. Should you decide to visit other areas, I have family all over the place. It is fine for me to stay with them. You can say that I am, 'at your beckon-call.' I will ensure your safety by never leaving the side of my charge."

He smiled a bright smile as he brushed her arm. Savannah began to understand him. He did not mean to be aggressive or fresh. It was comparable to someone who hugs everyone compared to the person who likes their space. She decided at that moment not to make a big deal out of her idiosyncrasy of not liking to be touched by strangers.

"Ms. Smith, may I introduce Maria? She also comes with the villa. She is your private cook and cleaner. If you want her to accompany you to the beach or shopping, Maria is also a great companion. You may desire to purchase her lunch now and then in return for her company. She will entertain you with her vast knowledge. Her wit is unparalleled. Yes, she will keep you laughing!" Gustus smiled brightly.

"Maria, I am delighted to meet you. We shall indeed have some outings together. Will you show me around? This place is divine."

Maria didn't move. She remained in the same spot holding a dish towel. Just like Gustus, she smiled from ear-to-ear. No one moved. Savannah looked at the caretaker questioningly.

"Oh, Maria only speaks Italian. Don't worry; you will pick it up quickly. Here is a book of our language which we provide for each of our guests. You are not the only one who arrives without learning the language."

Gustus looked at her as a teacher may stare-down a student who did not finish his homework. Savannah felt a little foolish.

"Oh, I'm sorry. I've been told that most Italians speak some English. It did not seem urgent that I learn the language."
"Ah, not a problem. The book will help. Isn't Maria lovely?"
Savannah looked again at the aging, dowdy Italian woman. She was as broad as tall with missing teeth. Still, her smile seemed contagious.
"Yes, she is stunning, indeed."
Savannah tired of all of the dialogue. She longed for a nice shower and nap.
"She is my aunt. I have many cousins here as well. You will be welcomed into our fold." Gustus refused to quiet. The tired woman only nodded.
"It's okay. I can explore the house myself. I'm sure that I can figure out where you want me to stay."
She walked away slightly confused but desperately in need of rest.
"Wrong. It is my pleasure to escort you everywhere. Let me show you the half of the house which is yours."

"Do you mean that I don't get the entire villa?"

The confused woman shook her head. The fees for the rental of this villa had been astronomical.

"No, you did not have a good travel agent if she told you that you paid for the entire home. I am sorry. You see, this villa has twelve rooms. It is in the most desirable location. You get the car, Maria, plus me. What did you expect?" He now seemed exasperated.

Savannah tired of all of this. Where was her room? Right now, that was the only thing of importance.

"Ms. Savannah, you rented one wing of the house. The owners keep the other side for themselves. They only come for a few months each year. They live in California most of the time. Let's begin with a tour of the entire house. Then I will show you the wing that is yours." It sounded as if this could last forever. Would the torture never end?

Savannah begrudgingly followed Gustus. The views from the owner's balcony took her breath away. The house nestled in the hug of a large hill and looked down on Peraggi beach. Today, the water was stunning. Shades of green mingled with dark blue colors all of which were topped by small white caps. Bright purple bougainvillea surrounded the terrace. Gentle winds blew the smells of the seaside into the villa. All of the doors and windows were opened. The freshness and coolness of the day seemed unforgettable.

"Gustus, you were correct once again. This place is the most stunning place on earth besides my beautiful house which is located in the New Orleans area." She smiled at that thought.

Gustus recited the long, impressive history of this villa. Savannah no longer felt tired but excited. How would her wing look?

"Now, the moment to which we have all been looking forward. Drum roll, please." Gustus made the sound of a fake drum roll. Savannah shook her head at the theatrical performance. Did he not understand how long she had traveled? Could he not display a small amount of compassion? The Italians must be a hardy bunch.

She knew better than to rush it. Rushing Gustus only prolonged whatever it was that he described when someone tried to hurry him. Savannah thought about suggesting that he reduce his television which may curb his dramatic ways. She did not. Instead, she obediently followed him as he picked up all of her things for the tenth time and led the way. Why had he not deposited these items in one central location instead of dragging them around?

Suddenly, Gustus pushed a set of double doors open. They looked ancient. Savannah couldn't wait to learn their history. All of the doors and windows of the villa stood framed with darkly stained arches. Her entrance hall floor appeared to be ancient mosaic tiles. Brightly colored fish and flowers welcomed her from their position in the beautiful tiles. All of the walls glowed in the late afternoon sun with a soft green stucco. A large flower arrangement of fresh red roses sat on an antique table. It was stunning.

Outside, blues, pinks, and oranges painted the sky. Silence surrounded the house on this, her first night.

The south-wing contained a large entrance, two bedrooms, two baths, two sitting rooms which were gigantic. An inside dining room and an outside one. A minuscule kitchen pleased Savannah. She smiled at Gustus.

"Of course, Madame, Maria will cook all of your meals. You have one dining room here."

They entered a sunny room with views of the beach. The day was almost spent. The American woman realized that she would experience sunsets each evening.

This place was more than she could ever have dreamed.

"Now, for the surprise! Follow me; please watch your step here." A broad smile greeted her as he pushed opened two more large doors revealing her private pool. It was surrounded by shrubs. There were large borders of bright purple bougainvillea surrounding the house. The feeling of absolute isolation thrilled her even though surrounding her were other mansions and their owners. She possessed the best of two worlds, people if she wanted or isolation. If she desired, she could remain nude all day.

*I'll paint nude by the pool as I look over Peraggi beach. What a way to spend my days!*

"If you desire, Madame, you could paint nude by the pool as you overlook the beach. Many women do this. I promise not to look unless you ask." Gustus smiled broadly.

"No, I'm not going to ask you for any such thing. Now, what time does Maria serve dinner? I would love to shower and rest before it is served."

Gustus looked shocked.

"Well, Madame, we are at your service." This statement seemed absurd since he had told her how to do everything but breathe since her arrival. Now, they were at her call? When did that occur? "Dinner is served whenever you desire. Do you prefer early or late dinners? Maria already cooked a large pot of sauce with pasta and salad for you this evening. Is that agreeable? She will prepare whatever you request in the future. My aunt is a gourmet chef. Her culinary talents will delight you."

"Please instruct Maria that I give her the authority to prepare anything that she wants for me. I am not a picky eater. In fact, I don't eat much. In answer to your question, I prefer to eat early. My swimsuits won't fit well if I over-eat. Will they?"

"Ah, so you are asking me to be the judge of this lovely body?" He pointed to her and smiled. "This request is indeed an honor. When do you propose that we have this 'beauty contest?'"

"My friend, you must give it up. This scenario will never happen."

Slowly, she closed the massive door in the face of another smile.

## THIRTY-TWO: FIRST DAY OF HEAVEN

Savannah quickly unpacked. One bag made everything so easy. Promptly, she arranged all of the beautiful books which she purchased earlier on one of the shelves. An entire library of the owner's books waited for her perusal on the many ledges. Maybe she shouldn't have purchased any books? There were plenty waiting for her. They appeared to be in many languages.
Fresh, coastal air filled the room. Smells of salt and seafood stirred her senses. In the backdrop of these aromas, someone grilled steaks. She realized that she hadn't eaten all day. Loudly, her stomach growled.
If the shower was any indication of the degree of perfection, the rest of the villa held, it was going to rate as heavenly. The water was steaming hot, just the way that she loved it. Waiting to enfold her aching body were massive, thick

white sheet towels. She wrapped one around her twice. Condensation covered the mirror by the window. Light gently reflected into the room where she stood mesmerized by the scene unfolding beneath her window. The sky appeared saturated with bright colors. All of the shades mixed in divine streaks of lavish tones. It was breathtaking!

Aromas of spices from Maria's sauce squeezed under the door to her room. Savannah's mouth salivated. She still had time for a quick nap. Tiredness ebbed over her not even allowing her to blow-dry her hair. Instead, she fell onto the highest bed she had ever witnessed. She could almost sleep standing up; it was such a tall bed.

Faces of other women refused to forgive her for what she had done. How many families had broken apart because of her selfishness? Cries of children called "Daddy, come home!"

He did not. Instead, he visited *Savannah's House*. Nights of paid-for-sex and liquor that flowed like water now bruised her conscience. Lots of cash spent for sex with beautiful women arranged by the selfish Madame. Savannah traded the security of wife and child for her greed. That money paid for her life of privilege. This trip to the Italian Riviera was paid for by sex-money.

Small children held out their tiny arms as they begged her to send their fathers back to homes where they were loved and needed. Instead, selfish men spent many long and expensive nights at *Madame Savannah's House.*

Poor **House** had no idea of the reputation which Susie Smith had given her. Once respected and loved, **House** was now a joke. A place of ill-repute would not welcome decent people. **House** received laughs and taunts instead. A once respected and loved home now was avoided by most. Savannah could feel **House** shake with rage when she finally understood what occurred in her shiny white walls. Maybe Savannah's mother and father had not behaved responsibly. Indeed, they were reprehensible. Still, her actions had betrayed the weakness of her spirit. Her behavior was not much better than the parents whom she detested. A person of strength would have risen above the mire. She should have graduated from college. There was an opportunity for her to make more of herself than a druggie.

Faces of classmates, long ago forgotten, paraded past. Friends who filled her days with laughter. Yes, they let her down, but her actions enticed them to continue on a downward spiral. She never bothered to try to uplift them. All of her problems, which she blamed on others, were created by none other than Susie Smith. No one else was to blame. When she faced that fact, she may be free of all of this old baggage.

Men, so many men were lovers. How many times did she lie? Nights filled with promises of love and devotion. Once they gave her money, she was gone. No wonder no one cared for her. She had never been worthy of that emotion. Yes, even the escape of love from her life was the result of her devious lies.

Over and over the faces paraded before her. Men, women, and children, especially the faces of innocent children whom she hurt and destroyed. Their number was unknown. Savannah longed to apologize. How could she ever repay the hurt that she caused so many?

Abruptly, she sat up in the giant bed. Darkness filled the room. There was no sound.

"**House**, what is wrong? Where am I?" Now, her screams filled the house. Horror raged in her soul. Was this Hell? "I deserve to be here. Please, please everyone forgive me." Was she losing her mind?

Loudly, her screams echoed in the empty room. She had no memory of her surroundings, only fear. Heavy knocking on the door surprised her. Savannah shook her head as she tried to remove the webs of panic and fear from the muffled feeling inside her head.

"Lovely lady, let me inside. Are you okay? Is there someone in your room? We heard screaming. You sound afraid. Let me in or I, Gustus, will break down the door."

Gustus, beautiful, wonderful Gustus: driver and gardener extraordinaire, yes, she now remembered.

Savannah opened the door with the towel wrapped snugly around her. Now she recalled it all; she was in heaven not hell.

"I am sorry. Probably all of the travel created fearful dreams for me. If I confused or upset you and Maria, I apologize. Is dinner ready? I'll be right down!"

The embarrassed guest dressed quickly for dinner. The earlier emotion shook Savannah's body. What horrible dreams consumed her in this place of peace and enchantment? She never experienced such horrific night thoughts when she was at **House**.

The terrified, embarrassed lady realized at that moment, the presence of another person in her life. Had He always been there?

Savannah had never been a religious person. She watched the dissension and hypocrisy in the churches and wondered how anyone could support them. Yes, Susie Smith was a sinner; maybe the worst sort of person but the religious fanatics were also wrong. That was what she always told herself when confronted by a church member. In her past, she ran from such encounters. For the first time, the realization that there existed a divine spirit which hovered around her stirred her soul. Had those horrible dreams caused a purging of her pain? Now, the rebellious Susie longed for a relationship with this figure of peace and light.

Pleasant aromas pulled her thoughts back to the present. There would be plenty of time to ponder her newly found awareness.

When she entered the kitchen, Maria stood over a pot of steaming pasta. The smells reminded the young woman that she had not eaten all day.

"Maria, I apologize for being late for dinner. Punctuality is one of my most prized attributes. Seldom am I late. This tardiness will not happen again."

Savannah smiled sweetly at the rotund woman holding a wooden spoon and dish cloth.

*Does she always carry a dishcloth?*

It appeared so. Maria stood in the same spot with the childish grin.

"Uh, Maria, did you hear me?"

"Madame, I have explained that my aunt does not understand English. You must study our book to communicate with her. Gustus will not always be hovering around to save you." Valiantly, he smiled as if he had pulled the guest from a burning building.

"Yes, of course, I forgot. This time has been an unusually tiring day for me. You must forgive me."

What the guest wanted more than forgiveness was a bowl of pasta and a glass of wine. Still, the tired guest sat down at the table which was set for two.

"Madame, please do not sit there. You have sat in the seat of the guest who is not here. Your space is over there."

Gustus pointed to the other empty place with a look of irritation.

Such silly actions rubbed the woman into a reaction.

"Now, you look here Gustus, I have paid a fortune to stay here. It is beautiful, and I am happy, but you seem to request ridiculous things of me. No, I will not move. This is my seat, right here, where I am sitting. If you and Maria want to set an empty place, which sounds absurd, go ahead. This place, right here, is mine." Savannah hit the table in front of her for effect.

Gustus appeared overwhelmed. The irritated look left his face. He briefly smiled.

"Madame, you bring all of this on yourself. We are not to blame." Savannah shook her head with confusion.

"You see, consistently, you apologize and ask us what you should do. We are not accustomed to such behavior. Maybe you should put us in our place by telling us what you want. That is the behavior which we expect. The extra place is for your 'French boyfriend'! When will he arrive?"

Maria turned to the stove as she spooned a hefty portion of the pasta. Savannah laughed gaily.

He was correct. Since her birth, Susie Smith had avoided confrontation except for the time when she phoned the travel agent with directions of her trip and

demanding that she wanted to leave "now, right now." Gustus and Maria had just propelled her into being the person of whom she dreamed. Now, she understood. Certain rules existed in the life of the privileged. She must learn these and act appropriately. There was so much to learn about being a lady.
"You are correct, Gustus about my subservient behavior. There will be no one joining me. Now, please serve me." Those words caused discomfort to the poor woman from the streets but delighted Gustus.
"Now, Madame, we understand!"
The gourmet dinner was not gourmet at all. Savannah gave it 2-stars but ate with gusto since nothing else was available.
"You see, my aunt is an excellent cook. Yes, everyone raves about her pasta which is her best dish."
Stunned, Savannah set the wine glass down a little too hard.
"This is her best? Well, tomorrow night, I would love to have a fresh fillet of

grilled fish. Tell her not to fuss over a sauce. Just plain, delicious fresh fish. Will you request this for me?" Gustus nodded excitedly.

"Madame, you will love Maria's fish. It will delight you!"

After dinner, Savannah strolled out to her private terrace. Sweet honeysuckle smells filled the darkened air. Night sounds of distant music from Peraggi beach added a happy feeling. Savannah considered that this was as good as her life could ever become. Hours peacefully passed. Savannah filled her wine glass from the bottle that Gustus brought to her. Maria had gone to bed right after dinner. Gustus sat faithfully by the light in the entrance foyer of the villa reading a newspaper in case she should need him.

Dreams filled her relaxed mind. Again, she walked in terrains of fertile soil which offered sweet smells of large, purple grapes. He held her hand. They stopped in front of a tortuous, gnarled olive tree. Gently, he stooped down and kissed her.

# THIRTY-THREE: LIFE IN PARADISE

Savannah had been so exhausted that she did not remember going to bed the night before, but she did recall the dreams which filled her head. Of course, they were of the Frenchman. Last night, in heavenly thoughts of slumber, she was introduced to the mother of the man who occupied her thoughts. It seemed that once, she laughed out loud at something that he said.

The shutters could not prevent the morning sunlight from streaming into the pretty room. Savannah sat up energetically. This was her first full time in Portofino. The exhausting trip from the day before ended well with sweet dreams. Today, what adventures would wait for the American in Paradise?

As she walked down the stone stairs of her villa, the ancient beauty of the structure struck her. Each detail in this first-class home had been laboriously perfected. All of the doors and windows opened to the fresh sea air just as they did yesterday.

Savannah tiptoed into the dining room. She could see Maria in the small kitchen. Ms. Smith had not looked at the Italian handbook last night so had no idea how to request her breakfast.

Gustus was not in sight. When the lady with the dishtowel saw her, she quickly entered with a bright smile and a pot of coffee.

Italian java delighted the taste buds of the guest. Outside the window, Gustus worked in the exquisite garden which filled with sweet aromas and beautiful, vibrant colors.

Somehow, the two women were able to communicate somewhat but not clearly enough. Savannah finally ran up the stairs to retrieve the book which Gustus provided on the day of her arrival. That did help a great deal. Although she struggled with pronunciations, the guest quickly caught on by listening to Maria pronounce her incorrect words. Soon,

Maria proudly carried a tray holding French toast lightly covered in confectioners sugar, steaming hot Italian syrup, and a serving of bacon. The American never ate a large breakfast, but this morning, her cravings were different. Everything was delicious. Maria seemed starved for company, so Savannah invited her to walk outside. They sat down in two chairs by the pool. Maria glowed with pleasure at being included with the guest. Talking with her was easy. The older woman was quick and funny. Together they laughed loudly until Gustus hurriedly joined them.
"Aunt Maria, you should not bother our guest. You are the help. Go back to your kitchen."
Savannah was surprised. Most likely, he felt the need always to be in control.
"Gustus, I invited your aunt. I enjoy her company."
Maria stood awkwardly possibly embarrassed by his chastisement.

"Maria, we will go to Santa Margherita soon. I will need your help as I shop." The American smiled at the Italian cook. Savannah spoke the Italian phrase easily. Gustus looked at her perplexed.

"I look forward to accompanying you, my lady. That assignment is my job." Savannah nodded and smiled. When the two staff members left her, the guest continued her walk out into the gardens. The variety of shrubs and flowers provided a lovely contrast in the smells and colors. Grape plants and orange trees added to the sensual aromas that silently lifted from the sunny garden. Not only were the smells delightfully stimulating to the olfactory senses, but the contrast of colors added pleasure to the sense of sight. Everything about the villa demanded study and also deep thought.

Soon, Savannah was drawn to the pool. Hastily, she ran up the stairs and returned wearing her swimsuit. The water of the pool was pristine.

Swimming briskly, the young woman forgot all thoughts as she basked in the hot sunshine.

She needed activity; she ran up the stairs to her room. Hurriedly, she changed her clothes. Then, she walked into the sitting room to find Maria dusting. Gustus entered the room. He was sweating from the heat of working outside in the gardens.

Even though she had never driven in another country, Savannah procured the keys to the Fiat. *Driving to the town of Santa Margherita should be simple enough. Anything must be better than the horrible driving of Gustus.*

The American tourist drove slowly down the steep hill as she winded her way into the crowded area. It was a nightmare. Now, she understood why Gustus had such problems. The tiny road was dirt with large rocks peering out. If anyone dared attempt entering from the opposite direction, it would be impossible to pass. Each inch of the way, she prayed for the road to remain empty. She should have trusted her driver instead of being critical of him. Once she finally arrived at the end of the road, Savannah realized the easiest way to continue was to leave the car and catch a shuttle to Santa Margherita. Things became easier once she stepped onto the passenger-filled shuttle. All around her, the sounds of foreign chatter spouted from smiling, happy faces. She loved the feeling of melting into the chaos. Being surrounded by others, yet totally isolated from communication, pleased her.

Many hours passed as she shopped in the busy tourist town of Santa Margherita. Fabulous, high-end shops kept her attention. It was fun being a woman of leisure with unlimited funds. She purchased several strappy swimsuits, sandals, and cover-ups. When she returned to the car, her arms filled with bags of treasures. Everything had seemed conveniently located. The inability to understand Italian had not prevented her from feeling secure and comfortable being on her own. The sales staffs were able to assist her since many of them did speak the English language. Tomorrow would be the day to visit Portofino.

Gustus arrived at the car just as his guest parked. She hugged the steering wheel and breathed a sigh of relief. The driver smiled. He understood her reaction. Driving from the villa to the water was treacherous and dangerous. Happily, he assisted her with the many shopping bags. The guest was relieved that he didn't pipe "I told you so."

The remainder of the day, Savannah set up her new easel and painted her first canvas. Gustus brought her lunch by the pool. An overcooked fillet of fish looked sadly at her. Maria must have been busy with other things. No matter, how could she find fault here?

For the rest of the day, Savannah lovingly added layers of bright colors:

purples, reds, pinks, and gold onto her canvas. Just before dinner time, she stepped back to admire her work. The resemblance to the south-garden was remarkable. Lovingly, Savannah carried her first attempt at being an artist back to the foyer so that it could continue to dry. Gustus waited in his chair by the lamp. He praised his charge for possessing such talents.

After a long, lazy nap, the guest bounded down the stairs prepared to be dazzled by a gourmet dinner. Instead, Maria served a hefty portion of meaty pasta. It was almost the same as last night's dinner which had failed to gain great reviews from the guest. After Maria had served her, she turned smiling as if expecting praise. Savannah looked at the thick, heavy meal with disappointment.

"Maria, we need to prepare a different dish. I am tired of the same pasta. Did you have a busy day?" The only response was a giant smile. Gustus rushed into the room.

"Now, see here Ms. Savannah, all of our guests love my aunt's pasta dishes. This fact is the reason that she fixed it again. Right, Maria?" Again the big smile as if she had delighted the shocked and slightly irate diner.

"Aunt Maria, our guest tires of the pasta. You must be shocked by such unbelievable words since most people request it night after night." He looked threateningly at Savannah.

The American doubted his words but refused to make her host angry. Instead, she began to eat the offering. It was delicious but a little too rich for the slim woman. She did not desire to become fat on this trip. Her dream had been delicious fish straight from the waters.

"Gustus, why don't I go early tomorrow morning to the beach? I'll bring back some fresh fish. I would love some large sea scallops." She smiled.

"Madame, you know not what you speak." He peered at her sternly.

"We refuse to allow you foreigners coming to our pristine waters and destroying them. You would probably be a victim of pirate fishing!"

*What is he ranting about now?*

Savannah doubted that such a thing existed.

"Gustus, I'll buy from locals. Don't worry."

"They **are** the pirate fishermen. You see, our people are guilty of fishing for profit without thoughts to the long-term effects of their actions. They fish in illegal, unlicensed vessels without following the environmental laws of our land. Did you know that it is not legal fishing for salmon, red tuna, and *datteri de mare*?"

"I'm sorry da what?"

"*Datteri de mare,* these are date mussels. They require a very long time to mature. They must not be removed until they are fully developed."

"That's fine; I don't want any date mussels. I want regular ones and dreamy scallops! See, I'm capable of purchasing healthy, legal fish." She issued a big smile.

"Really? What others do you love? You are correct; you can easily and legally purchase *cozze*."

"I don't want any strange fish. Cozze is not on my list."

"Oh, you don't desire regular mussels? How about *gamberetto* or cod? Do oysters, turbo and squid interest you? You probably don't wish for *capanta* either?"

"No, none of that strange stuff interests me. Some beautiful sea scallops are my desire for dinner tomorrow. Maybe oysters or shrimp on a bed of lettuce with some spectacular dressing for lunch." Savannah's mouth watered with delight.

"Ah ha! Capanta, these are sea scallops as well as gamberetto are shrimp. Madame, you require Gustus to

accompany you for your fresh fish tomorrow. I'll drive you early before breakfast. How can you purchase fish when you don't understand what you are buying? Eventually, you will be able to shop alone but not yet. Just as you learned the difficulty of driving here, you will experience problems with the fishermen. You could get into some serious trouble. Please trust Gustus."
In her mind, the American had started keeping score of who won the most arguments between herself and her host. Although her companion could be irritating, she enjoyed sparring with him. After dinner, Savannah carried the rest of her wine bottle outside. The wines which were served to her each day were spectacular. Each night, a different concoction waited for her approval. She had begun to carry the bottle outside so that she could compile a list of her favorites. The problem was that each one was delicious. Without thinking, the woman hugged herself gently.

The nightly garden smells soothingly offered evening wares of jasmine and other heavenly delights. Down on the beach, the music geared up for a long night. Here, she sleepily dozed in her piece of heaven. Stars filled the skies above. They blurred quickly enough as her eyes became heavy in the thick, salty air. The hand of Gustus gently shook her.

"Madame, is it not the time for bed? I tire easily now. Do you mind? I don't feel comfortable allowing you to stay here alone."

Sweet Gustus, her driver, gardener, procurer of fresh fish, and now, guardian. It may be difficult leaving him at the end of her time here.

## THIRTY-FOUR: DAY AFTER DAY

Early the next morning, before dawn, there was a loud knock on her door. Savannah awakened confused. Why would anyone wake her before daylight? Then she remembered asking Gustus to take her down to the beach for the shopping of fresh seafood. Was she insane? She groaned.
"You told me to wake you, Ms. Savannah. We should be going. The fish are calling us!"
He began to sing some stupid song in Italian.
Savannah pulled on a beach cover-up over her underwear and stepped into her sandals. Breathlessly, she opened the door.
Gustus looked sparkling as he stood before her. Dressed in his usual attire of cream linen slacks and white shirt with a straw fedora, he appeared dapper. As they walked outside into the fresh, early morning light, he looked as if he was the

renter and she the help. Again, Savannah groaned.

"I hope Maria appreciates this. Maybe today, the fish will be deliciously prepared without being dried out." She meant nothing unkind with her comment.

Gustus glared at her but did not respond. The guest never considered how her words must sound to the protective nephew.

Carefully, he drove the red Fiat convertible down the steep hill. Lights already glowed from some of the residences.

*What tourist rises this early? These must be homeowners.*

When they stopped at the beach, Savannah came to life with the sights before her. Many fishermen proudly stood as they displayed the nightly catch. The smells, of fresh seafood mixed with the aromas from the Mediterranean Sea, were divine. The American wished that she could remember this feeling forever. Gustus spied someone whom he recognized. Speedily, he steered her in the direction of his friend.

"Marcus is the best fisherman. He would never fish in areas where he should not nor deliver an under-par catch."

The fisherman smiled broadly as the two men embraced. There wasn't a tooth in the mouth of Marcus, but dark eyes sparkled at her from a wrinkled and very tanned face. Savannah nodded as she pointed at some delicious fresh oysters, shrimp, and mussels.

"Ms. Savannah, we can't eat all of this today. The purpose of 'fresh' is that it is 'fresh.' We can come back tomorrow."

"Nonsense, we can refrigerate it and eat it tomorrow. I'm certain that Maria will prepare it correctly tonight. I've decided to go into Portofino shopping today. Will you join me?"

Gustus shrugged at the fisherman who did not appear to understand any of their English words. Instead, the Italians chatted softly together. Happily, Marcus accepted payment from Gustus for the fish.

"You realize that the little town of Portofino only has four hundred and seventy-nine residents, but there may be hundreds of shoppers this time of year especially with the large cruise ships and tourists. Are you sure that you need to go there? Shopping is terribly expensive." He did not look happy with her.

"Gustus, come on, I must see the city. I don't mind the prices. Come on; I'll buy your lunch."

"What about Aunt Maria? She would love to accompany you. Wouldn't you prefer her company?"

Already the two individuals argued like a brother and sister. He appeared to bait her often.

"No, I want you to accompany me. You are much more sophisticated." She flashed her brightest smile.

He did not look pleased as he carefully drove back up the treacherous hill. The wind blew strongly adding to the dangerous condition.

They drove past a large park which welcomed residents. That place would provide another day's diversion with walking paths offering exercise options instead of her usual twelve laps of swimming alone in the lovely pool. Savannah realized that some of the precious time of her vacation had already passed. She did not want this time to end. Gustus parked the car as Savannah rushed her fresh fish inside to the waiting cook.

"Maria, what French toast again? I was hoping for fresh fruit today."

Maria stood smiling with a large platter of the meal Savannah enjoyed yesterday. Savannah sighed.

"Diversity, Maria, you must learn diversity."

Her tone divulged the irritation which she felt. She plopped down at the dining room table as Gustus wrapped the fish for storage in the fridge. Maria looked at him with confusion but continued to smile.

Hungrily, Savannah gorged on the delicious breakfast. Maybe it did not represent diversity, but it was one meal that Maria prepared to perfection. The guest noticed Gustus watching her. He almost spoke but turned and walked away. After gulping down three cups of coffee, Savannah rushed upstairs for a shower so that she and Gustus could leave for her shopping expedition. She heard him and Maria softly speaking downstairs. When she returned, they continued to speak in Italian so that she could not understand a word of their conversation.

Savannah and her driver entered the convertible without talking.

"Gustus, will you tell Maria that we won't be back for lunch? I'm going to buy yours today. Remember?"

He did not smile but softly spoke, "I've already told her not to expect us until dinner time."

Savannah was too excited to be concerned with her staff. What could she possibly have done to upset them now? Any concerns, she hastily pushed from her mind.

Gustus appeared distracted as he drove the few minutes drive from Paraggi Beach to Portofino. Immediately, Savannah felt at home. Before her stretched some of the most high-dollar stores in the world. This *woman from the streets* had quickly learned to enjoy the best in the world. Gustus followed her around without commenting. She knew that he was pouting over her remarks about his aunt. The guest tired of always apologizing for one thing and then another. As the time passed, he began to relax, and his smile returned.

Savannah only made a few purchases. There was not any reason to buy clothes which she didn't need. Plenty of nice shops waited back in New Orleans. Soon, she tired of the crowds and the heat.

"Gustus, do you know any quiet restaurants? We need shade and coolness."

Her dress was soaked from perspiration while Gustus's shirt looked as if he just stepped outside from the air conditioning.

*How does he do it?*

Without a saying a word, Savannah felt his hand guiding her arm down the street. His large smile greeted all whom they met. Many people seemed to know him. Softly, he guided her inside a dark, almost cold restaurant. It felt wonderful as it provided not only coolness from the heat but darkness from the bright light. The restaurant's ambiance produced instant relaxation on the many patrons who seemed to be quietly dining on something wonderful. Savannah couldn't help it; her thoughts returned to Maria's cooking. No matter how kind she tried to be to her, the results from the cook's attempts were pretty awful.

Just as she started to share her concerns, a cute young waitress walked sexily to their table. Quick Italian remarks passed between the driver and the young woman. Obviously, they knew each other well. She mentioned Maria as her eyes darted nervously to Savannah. Something was going on with Gustus's aunt but what?

"Gustus, will you order for me? A nice fillet of fresh, local fish which isn't overcooked and dried out would be fantastic."

Again, concerned looks passed between Gustus and his friend. It appeared that the Italian woman could understand English, but she refused to recognize the American. The young woman refused to look Savannah's way. Quickly, he ordered for them. Then he smiled at Savannah.

"Have I told you that you look 'Bella' today?"

It seemed that he attempted to distract her from the earlier conversation and looks which passed between him and his friend, Gabriella.

"Thank you. You obviously know our waitress well. Did I notice a little flirting?"

She refused to say anything which may upset him. The constant theatrics with him tired her.

They enjoyed a chilled Rose´ wine with the scrumptious meal of fish and delicious local vegetables. The meal tasted light and healthy. Savannah bit her tongue as she wanted to say, "If only Maria could prepare food this well." Instead, she said nothing. The two people enjoyed a long and lazy lunch. Most of the other patrons had already left as she and her driver completed their wine. When they finally paid the bill and exited, Gabriella looked intently at Gustus, waved, then disappeared without a look in Savannah's direction.

Her driver made the trip back fun as they casually drove down the winding road by the Mediterranean. High winds coupled with a narrow street on an extremely high hill kept Savannah's eyes nervously glued to the path ahead. One mistake and the result could be fatal. While they drove back to the villa, she decided that her time spent with her paints and books as she relaxed safely at home ranked even more desirable than shopping in the heat and crowds.

Hours had passed since lunch, which had been a light one, so the guest felt famished as she entered the house. As she passed the kitchen with her packages, she spied Maria preparing a lovely salad. Would it be topped with fresh mussels, oysters, or shrimp? She salivated uncontrollably.

"Hi, Maria here is a package for you. Look, I have purchased a cookbook on the correct preparation of seafood. The secret appears to be not to overcook it. I hope that you aren't offended by this?"

The resident thrust the Italian cookbook into the small woman's face who continued to smile warmly. Gustus looked at the guest unhappily.

"Ms. Savannah, surely, you know that my aunt is doing her best. Can't you be happy with her efforts?"

"Look, Gustus, I'm glad that you mentioned this. I paid for a gourmet chef, but that is not what I have received. It is not my wish to upset you or Maria, but I feel that the owner should be alerted as to what is transpiring here. It is impossible for me to believe that other renters have not expressed the same thing." She quickly turned and walked away.

After a quick nap and long shower, Savannah walked briskly back into the kitchen. Maria brightly smiled while she presented a blue plate which held freshly mixed greens topped with shrimp and oysters. The aroma which greeted the weary traveler created a sweet smile.

"This is what I mean. Maria, it looks great."

Gustus appeared relieved. He poured one of his finest wines. Slowly, she lifted the fork to her mouth expecting a lightly sautéed crustacean delight. What her taste buds experienced was another overcooked mess. The oysters and shrimp reeked with overcooked nothingness. Any taste was destroyed by the same element which ruined each meal except breakfast. Poor Savannah tried to control her tongue but was unable.

"This is terrible. What is wrong with you, Maria? All that I requested was a salad topped with fresh seafood. This meal is once again over-prepared. I refuse to eat it. I'm going to call the owner tomorrow. I know that she lives in Nevada now. She needs to understand the degree of incompetency being forced on her guests. It is beyond me how rentals can continue so briskly with food such as this. Never mind, I'll just starve while I'm here. At least, you should consult the cooking book. You need help!"

Gustus looked upset as he sat down at the table. He held his head in his hands. Everything else was correct. The table settings were perfect. Long-tapered candles greeted the guest each evening as did the finest wines. Soft opera music in the background was conducive to a relaxed state. Maria's cooking ruined it all.

Savannah longed to sit by the pool as had become her custom each evening but felt too angry to be in the presence of Gustus and his aunt. Instead, she turned on the sound system and enjoyed one of the owner's opera recordings. While reading the latest book, her temper calmed. Before long, she regretted her earlier outburst. Tomorrow, she would apologize and make things right. It was never her intention to telephone the owner.

## THIRTY-FIVE: TOO LATE

*The sting of words spoken in anger and haste can never be recalled.*
All through the long night, Savannah heard the words of an old friend who died of a drug overdose in her youth. She missed Sam and his funny ways. Never had Sam been unkind to anyone. His demons killed him, but his memory burned brightly in the heart of the woman who called him "friend." Suddenly, he was gone.
Often Savannah recalled the last night they were together. Out-of-control words poured from her mouth. Now, she could not remember what had transpired between them. Only the mean statements which she yelled at him. The next morning, when she learned that Sammy died, the young girl was devastated.
Last night, Savannah stayed up way into the evening. Possibly her motive was to irritate the driver and his sister with her

overly loud music. The guest wasn't sure where they lodged in the house but knew that they did have living quarters inside the large, rambling structure. Although she calmed down as she read her book and soaked in the majestic melody of *Madame Butterfly*, it was difficult not to retaliate against Maria and Gustus. After all, she had not received all that had been promised to her.

As a result of her immature actions last evening, this morning presented a problem for her. Instead of her usual early hour, she slept way into the morning almost to lunch. She felt embarrassed facing the two Italians. They must think her weak and silly. Awake but unwilling to face them, she was forced to run downstairs when she heard the commotion.

*The sting of words spoken in anger and haste can never be recalled.* Over and over those words burned in her mind.

The loud sounds were disruptive and frightening. It all began with loud banging on the door which was followed by pitiful wails. The sound was blood curdling; it was a dreadful transaction unfurling somewhere in the house. By the time Savannah dressed and ran into the kitchen, many loud voices assaulted the typically peaceful space. Nowhere in sight was Maria or Gustus.

As the American stood watching strangers, who kept arriving, thrashing around in the usually quiet area, she understood that something terrible happened to Gustus and his aunt. Unsure of what else to do, she remained glued to her spot by the sunny, kitchen window where Maria usually stood as she prepared a meal for her guest. Dread filled the soul of the ungrateful woman who said such silly, mean statements last night to the two people whom she had come to love. Had she again killed someone whom she loved by hasty, stinging words?

Savannah remained standing in the same spot, while other strangers continued to arrive. They all seemed to know each other. No one looked at the foreign guest. It was impossible for her to understand what transpired but she was certain that it involved Maria. Her name was repeated over and over. Then the sound of "Maria" was followed with the uncontrollable wails.

Amazingly, after about thirty minutes of this, she heard the siren of an emergency vehicle. Her legs gave way beneath her. She collapsed to the floor. Tears ran uncontrollably from her brown eyes. Many rushed to assist her, but she motioned them away. It was better to remain crouched to the side of the sink than trying to stand. She remained there. The siren grew close and then departed. Savannah could not stand. To her amazement, Gustus entered the room. To see him broke her heart. His usual dapper countenance appeared disheveled. His bright smile departed.

The dark hair stood on end from the top of his head. His bright, brown eyes seemed almost swollen closed. His clothing was soiled and wrinkled. Savannah watched him as his eyes quickly surveyed the room. When he witnessed her crouched alone in the corner, he rushed to her side. He pulled her off the floor and into his arms. Again, the sounds of the earlier wails reeked from his throat. He pulled her away as he looked intently into her face. Fear showed in his eyes. She could only wait. No sound came from her.
"Do you understand what has happened? Maria is gone. It is so unbelievable that we will never see her again. My beloved aunt is dead."
Savannah shook her head with shock. She pulled him into her face again. Finally, she found her voice.
"How could this be? What has happened? Did someone hurt her?"
Gustus shook his head sadly. Then he turned to the others. Gently, he spoke to

them in the language that they shared. Slowly, they walked in front of her. Each nodded to her respectfully, but they did not speak as they began to leave. Moments passed until they all left. She and Gustus stood alone in an embrace.

"What I'm about to tell you will cause you great pain. You must understand that no one blames you. I am the blame, not you. Please remember that over the next few days, if you decide to return to the states, I will understand. You may never desire to see my face ever again. I will support whatever decision that you make."

He walked her to the table where they sat facing each other. He took her hands as he began to speak again. Sadly, he looked into her very soul.

"Ms. Savannah, you were always correct. My Maria was not a gourmet chef. She raised me when my parents were killed in an accident. She always loved me just as she did her five children. We were poor. They barely made enough to take care of themselves, but they gladly accepted me. Never did I feel different from the others. Aunt Maria was a homemaker from a rustic family of hard workers. The real gourmet chef is Annabella, my cousin." Tears forced him to stop the story. He gained his composure.

"Do you desire food? I can prepare your breakfast."

Savannah considered never eating again; certainly, she had no appetite at this point. When she shook her head, he stood and poured a cup of coffee for each of them.

"This is the last thing that Aunt Maria will ever fix for us. She made the coffee early this morning as she studied the cookbook which you gave her last night." Again, his voice seemed to leave as he choked with emotion.

Carefully, almost robotically, he recited the remainder of the story. Maria determined to offer her guest a meal which she hoped may prevent Savannah from phoning the owner of the villa. When the aunt realized that she did not have the spices required, she decided to walk to the next estate. Gustus worked in the back of the garden outside of her view. He remained unaware of his aunt's actions. Poor Maria attempted to walk down the spiraling, steep road in the heat of the morning. Not only did she fall as she stepped over the large rocks, the medics believed that she suffered a heat stroke. When a neighbor saw her fall, he ran to her side, but she was gone. All of the primal yells and cries were friends and neighbors who witnessed what occurred.

Sadly, the two friends looked intently at each other. In her mind, she believed that she had caused Maria's death. Once again, a friend died due to her selfishness. She grabbed her friend, "Dearest Gustus, it is not your fault; it is mine. I killed her because of my selfish anger."

Again, he began to cry.

"You haven't heard the entire story. You see, my cousin, Annabella, is the chef here. She should have been present for your arrival. You would have been impressed with her culinary skills. Her latest pregnancy proved difficult. It became imperative for her to remain in bed at the end. This event occurred right before you arrived."

Gustus finished his story by explaining that he asked Maria to live in a small apartment inside the villa while his cousin recovered from the birth of her second child. Memories of the wonderful meals which his aunt cooked for him as a child had convinced him that Maria would be okay until his cousin's return. Of course, he was a poor child, so Maria's food tasted good enough. Annabella's family needed the money, so Aunt Maria covered for her. Maybe it was a little dishonest, but they thought that no one would be upset. The real chef was scheduled to return next

week. Things might have been fine if the guest had not become angry and demanded better. Then, Maria decided to walk so that she could obtain the required spices. She died trying to please their guest. His words hung in the thick air between them. Desperately, they clutched each other's hands. Naturally, they remained in shock most of the day. Gustus made funeral plans and phoned family as well as friends during the afternoon. Later, Savannah sat by the peaceful waters of the pool when a small old Opel Vivaro barely puttered into the driveway. A gorgeous, young woman jumped out with a familiar smile. It was the same smile that Maria wore each day. Savannah felt pulled to the girl as if she was a magnet.
"Hello, may I help you?"
"Ciao, I'm Annabella, the cousin to Gustus. Is he here? You must be the American. I understand that Maria's cooking did not suffice?"
Savannah broke out in tears.

*So, the entire family blames me. They hate me.*

"Oh, Don't cry! We understand. Maria possessed many talents, but cooking wasn't one. No one blames you. You got a bad deal from us. I'll make it up to you. The rest of your meals will delight you. I promise." There did not appear to be sadness in Annabella's countenance. Annabella appeared so light and happy that her attitude confused Savannah. Shouldn't she be sad and crying? This joyful countenance did not make sense. The American said nothing.

Gustus ran into the small arms of his cousin. His tears soaked the blouse of the newly arrived family member who hugged him tightly and smiled. She turned back to the American.

"In our country, the men are usually more emotional than the women. The way I see this, Aunt Maria lived a long and happy life. What more can any of us expect? I believe that we should celebrate such extraordinary people

when they leave us. She would not want tears. No, not Maria, she would desire a happy remembrance of her time here on this earth. She is in a better place."
Gustus instantly stopped the sobs as he finally restrained himself.
"Dearest Annabella, you are correct. I'm most happy that you are here. Savannah blames herself while I know that I am the cause of Maria's death."
"You are both selfish. Do you think that you are so vital that you caused the death of an individual with your thoughts? Neither of you can accomplish such great acts. Only God can do that. Lighten up with yourselves before you both have strokes. Life is to be enjoyed. Right?"
Boldly, she walked between Savannah and Gustus who looked at each other with opened mouths.
The short haired beauty with red spiked hair seemed to float as she walked familiarly into the sunny kitchen. Instantly, she opened the fridge and

began to assemble food in preparation for their next meal.

"Anyone hungry for lunch at this late hour or should we just plan on dinner?" The two shocked people again looked at each other. Suddenly, joy had entered their lives. Someone was in control. It was wonderful. Savannah felt exhausted. She excused herself for a nap while Gustus explained that they preferred to wait for dinner. He also excused himself. Dinner that evening was over-the-top in excellence. The fish, which they purchased earlier, was expertly cooked in a fish stew filled with the freshest ingredients. The salad which Savannah loved greeted her taste buds with freshness and popping flavors. The Roquefort cheese dressing was the best she had ever tasted. A Cabernet wine which Gustus poured had never tasted more exquisite because he served it with a smile.

The next week was filled with celebrations of a kind and thoughtful life well-lived. Smiles mixed with tears made acceptance of their loss more palatable. The bond between the driver and the American grew stronger and deeper.

Savannah again painted in the mornings. Annabella accompanied her on shopping expeditions and empowered her with local knowledge. Together, the two women walked trails in the park close to the villa. They became as inseparable as sisters. Gustus lighted with gladness when he saw them laughing and hugging with glee. Life was joyful again because an extraordinary young woman entered their presence. Annabella returned home to her children each evening but arrived before Savannah rose the next morning. The sound of the old Opel sputtering up the hill brought smiles to the guest.

## THIRTY-SIX: NEED FOR A CHANGE

Thoughts of dear Maria now brought a smile instead of tears. The loss of her life glued the remaining three together with a resolve to enjoy and celebrate just being alive. Now, they understood that each day was a blessing from God; it was not to be taken for granted. Savannah developed a spiritual side. The awareness of death carried to her the realization that much more existed than the people around her. What held everything and everyone was a powerful love from the Creator of the Universe. She soaked in His presence each day. A love and a strong bond developed not only for the three survivors but for the God whose presence they felt. Together, the three attended mass at the church which Maria had served and deeply loved. Often, they discussed this God as they enjoyed a beautiful sunset. Through it all, the memory of the handsome Frenchman never left her mind or heart. He seemed so real almost a sacred feeling. Thoughts of him brought Savannah comfort. It felt as if they were destined to be together. She didn't know how or when but felt sure that it would occur. Often, the American talked to her Heavenly Father. If only He would intervene and bring them together.

One day, she painted her beautiful art alone by the pool. Sometimes, she and Annabella enjoyed the pastime together. Lately, the two women had begun to sell their art at the local market. Locals and tourists grabbed their wares as if starved for beautiful paintings. The women enjoyed meeting different people at the outdoor markets. Most days, they laughed away long, lazy hours. Frequently, the young woman brought her children for a visit. Savannah secretly regretted that she never had a family. Never, had she disclosed this to anyone.

Gustus approached Savannah one afternoon as she completed another painting.

"Aren't you ready for a road trip? Annabella's youngest will have a birthday soon. This time would be perfect for us to take that trip to Provence. Remember, you expressed a desire to go there when you first arrived? Something about a French boyfriend? I'm surprised that he has never visited you here." He smiled broadly.

"Gustus, I never said that, although it would be wonderful visiting such a famous place. It saddens me to think that my time here is over half-way complete. I shall miss you when I depart." Their eyes met briefly.

"Well, we knew our time would end. Let's keep Annabella's philosophy to celebrate life. We'll find joy from our departing each other."

Savannah wasn't sure that she understood his meaning, but the thought of visiting Provence stirred intrigue within her.

"Annabella has a friend who plans trips for our guests. Do you wish her advice?" Such a plan seemed too confining to Savannah.

"I would prefer that you and I just go. Do you anticipate problems finding lodging? Which part should we see? I want to visit a great winery; see fields of lavender; taste fresh thyme; smell juniper; cook with rosemary; study Cézanne, Matisse, and fall in love with fields of sunflowers just like Van Gogh! When do we leave? What sort of wardrobe do I need?"

Gustus laughed like old times. He grabbed her arms.

"Let's leave early tomorrow morning. What do you think?"

"Well, that's a little sudden. Don't we need to do something? I mean, can we just leave?"

"Why not? I have never seen you this animated. So, you are a spontaneous

American? I always thought that they were boring and predictable. I'll meet you at the bottom of the stairs at 5 am tomorrow morning."

He suddenly turned on his heel and was gone. Over his shoulder, he yelled, "I've got to meet a date on the beach. Ciao."

Savannah could hear merry laughter coming from the kitchen.

"I'll prepare an early dinner so that you two can get to bed sooner." Their chef loudly announced from the kitchen.

The American strolled into the kitchen mischievously.

"Your cousin has a date. Maybe it will be a late night for him? Perhaps, he is meeting the waitress Gabriella?" Annabella smiled wickedly.

"I doubt it. Gustus is gay. He meets a few friends at a restaurant on the beach. He always refers to that as his 'date.'" She smiled sadly.

"He would have been an incredible father, what a shame."

Quickly, she returned to her preparations.

Savannah walked outside into the gardens. She was not surprised by Annabella's news. Gustus seemed different. These latest facts did not change her love for the Italian. Could a more perfect place exist anywhere than right here? Were they making a mistake adding another country onto their schedule? Longingly, her thoughts returned to **House**. She experienced sadness when her mind visited the place that she loved the most; she would be relieved to arrive back at her home. Maybe Gustus and Annabella would visit her there?

The American tourist spent the remainder of the day enjoying the sunshine. How would the sun and light differ in Provence? This trip was a dream. All of her life, pictures of Van Gogh's sunflowers or Cézanne's famous mountain intrigued her. At the same time, ideas of the glitzy Italian Riviera had inspired her. She may not have been born with class, at least according to her mother, but Susie Smith stood on the threshold of fulfilling yet another childhood desire of traveling between the Italian and French Riviera.

She and Annabella enjoyed a delicious dinner of bruschetta covered with ripe figs, Gorgonzola, and other aged cheeses. The main entre´ of spinach and prosciutto stuffed veal rolls would cause her mouth to water for years to come. The two women picked one of Gustus's best wines. It served him right for deserting them for his friends.

Annabella freely discussed her cousin. He had earned many awards for his gardens especially his roses. With love, she shared the details about the death of his parents as well as the battles in middle-school. Although he did not appear feminine, he had always been considered different. Proudly, she detailed the way that he handled battles over being gay and turned them into something good. They both agreed that Gustus held a piece of their hearts. Savannah grew tired. She excused herself and prepared for bed. While waiting for slumber to pull her into herself, thoughts of Gustus filled her mind. At one time, she feared that he might be interested romantically in her. Sometimes, he touched her hand or looked so intently that she felt uncomfortable around him. She now realized that she did not need to fear his intentions. Besides, her heart was destined for another. *He* came to her thoughts without effort.

Each night, new repetitive thoughts caused sleep to wrap her peacefully inside arms of comfort. They walked in fields of lavender. Cézanne's mountain always stood in the back of her dream. Soft laughter escaped from the mouth of the American. She had studied too many art books. For a man such as he to be interested in her that would be the creation of a fairy tale. Seldom did Susie

Smith encounter painful memories of childhood horrors anymore. After she had become aware that God was always around her, all of the old misery was buried. Her life now seemed to exist on a different plane. Happiness and goodness surrounded her. Had God freed her from the bonds of pain created by a dysfunctional, abusive childhood? Tonight, her dreams took on a new dimension. She and the handsome French man walked fields of resinous shrubs outlined with lavender holding the hands of a small blonde girl. The laughter of the child caused Savannah to hug herself gently. A smile of innocence kissed her lips. It was the kiss of a small, golden girl.

# THIRTY-SEVEN: PROVENCE

As they drove with the wind in their faces while the darkness surrounded them, they looked at each other with contentment. Anyone who saw them would think that they were an old married couple. It seemed strange driving in the darkness with the top down.
"What do you want to do if we get a little rain? Should I put the top up or do you want to wait until it becomes a deluge?"
"Wait."
They smiled at each other as the salty air blew into their nostrils with increasing velocity.
"Gustus, this is divine. Are we dreaming? It doesn't get better than this."
"I agree."
The morning darkness turned into vivid streaks of red, pink, and gold.
"God's palette."

Gustus squeezed her hand.
"You know, if you weren't gay, we would be quite a couple." She smiled.
"I've thought of that but what can I say. You know that I love you. Still, I am what I am."
"I know."
The traffic began to increase as the feeling of divineness dissipated. The temperature remained pleasant despite the increase in heat as the sun claimed its location high in the summer sky. Soon, the waters disappeared as they moved more inland. The scenery was unforgettable.
"I wish that I could stop and paint it."
"You can. Shall I pull over?"
Savannah laughed.
"I'll wait for Provence. The lavender fields must create breathlessness?"
"They do."
So the drive went as they crossed the Italian border and drifted into France.
"I don't see a difference."
"In what?"

"Scenery."
"What did you expect?" He laughed with joy.
Savannah considered how easy it was spending time with a person like Gustus. Her thoughts captured her mind with images of her French dream man. Would he be this easy as they shared company? They walked in fields of lavender in her mind. He held her hand. Lately, it seemed that all thoughts of him also contained a white-haired girl. Her delicate frame grabbed at the heart of the woman. The child's white hair and blue eyes created a bond almost as mother and daughter. Savannah named the girl "Melissa."
"What are you thinking? I've never seen you look this happy."
"I'm not talking. You would laugh at me."
"Come on. Have I ever laughed at you?" They both giggled with glee because Gustus laughed at her frequently.

On and on, they contentedly drove. There were spells of rain, but they refused to put the top up until there was a "deluge." Gustus pointed out famous places to Savannah as they crossed into Monaco.

"Gustus, let's combine our funds and live here."

"I'm afraid that won't work since my funds don't compare to yours. I would never do that to you. I prefer to remain a dear friend."

After only four hours, Gustus pulled the car into a posh hotel.

"We have arrived, my Queen."

"It's funny that such a short drive could make me tired. Have you stayed here before?"

"Yes, many times. You will love it. Welcome to the Aix-en-Provence. Les Lodges Sainte Victorie is a four-star hotel. I made reservations in a suite. I don't think that my presence will threaten you from the adjoining room? We don't need to drive anymore. Once we turn the keys over to the valet, we are "home." The dining room is a Michelin one-star. Sound acceptable to my Queen?"

"Please, marry me." They smiled at each other.

Each grabbed a small bag as they entered the opulent hotel. Other tourists turned with interest to the handsome couple. Gustus held her little hand. When they entered the posh suite, they both ran for the extra-large bed.

"It's mine!"

"No, I made the reservations, it's mine."

"Let's share it."

Their laughter stopped.

"Whoa, we are getting out of control. I love you but no need to be reckless. See that sofa in the other room? That's mine, but I'll be close if you need me. Are you going to read for a while? I'll probably go outside and check out the pool." Gustus walked to his bag and awaiting swimsuit.

"We are just like a married couple. You know my schedule well."

Savannah closed the door separating the rooms with a naughty grin. He laughed. Instead of reading, she decided to explore, but Gustus had already left for the pool so he would be unable to join her. They probably needed their separate time. She didn't want to drown him in her need for attention. Savannah changed shoes and walked outside.

As she stepped outdoors, she automatically hugged herself. The beautiful people were out in droves. Usually, the old tugs of intimidation made her want to retreat from the biting words of people who represented the middle-school meanies but not anymore. The hug reinforced her self-worth. Savannah walked to the pool. Gustus talked with a handsome man as they shared a drink by the pristine, blue waters. He saw her and waved but did not invite her to join them. She widely smiled as she walked around the resort.

No detail had been overlooked in the building or landscaping.
Immediately, she began to search for her dream man. This action may sound foolish, but she knew that they were destined to be together. Never, had Savannah been surer of anything in her life. It must be this trip which would bring them together. She searched each face for his. Every child who passed was inspected for white hair and blue eyes. There were a few who met the description, but none were her future family. Hours passed. She tired. Defeatedly, the tourist, returned to the empty room.
After a quick shower, she turned down the thermostat and grabbed her current book. With great pleasure, she floated beneath the ironed sheets. Sleep came quickly. The sound of Gustus entering the room went undetected.
A few hours later, there was a gentle knock.

"My Queen, it is almost dinner time. Would you prefer that I make reservations for later?"

His voice sounded comforting. Even during such a short time apart, Savannah missed her friend and companion.

"No way! I'm famished. I'll be right there."

In less than fifteen minutes, they entered the dining room. A cheery room greeted them. It filled with happy diners who softly talked over candles and bottles of wine. Fragrant aromas of thyme, rosemary, and basil greeted the starving couple.

"Have I told you that you look stunning? That dress is beautiful on you."

"Thanks. Honestly, it is a fancy beach cover-up but who could tell?"

Gustus took her hand. They looked into each other's eyes with love. It was not the usual love, but it was theirs. The meal was unforgettable. Afterward, they strolled by the pool. The smell of chlorine entered their nostrils with a bit of a sting. Still, they sat on one of the chaise lounges. It was too early for bed. Music from the dining room wafted into their space. Gustus took her hand and pulled her onto his chest. Gently, they danced over and over to the words which Savannah did not recognize. Sometimes, he would sing the song to her in English. She vowed never to forget this moment. Would the Frenchman be so kind? Gustus watched her.

"Right there. You were thinking about whatever dominates your thoughts lately. Please confine in me. I would tell you if something created such intense desire for me. What is this place or maybe it is a person?"

He walked her back to their chairs. As they sat, two other couples joined them by the pool. They began to dance romantically together.

Gustus laughed softly.

"We are trendsetters, no?"

"My dearest friend, I long to tell you the desires of my heart, but they are so far-fetched that I fear you will laugh at me." Of course, he insisted that she share as he assured her that there would be no jokes or laughter. Carefully, she poured out her heart. The Frenchman had made such a profound impression on her. Gustus listened with great interest. She even described the little girl vividly to him. When she finished the story, she expressed a desire that the American woman and Frenchman must share their lives together. It was sure to happen. Gustus looked at her sadly.

"I experienced a similar situation in my life many years ago. I looked for him many years before I realized that it was only a dream not at all destined. Much pain resulted in the time I invested. The only outcome was a profound disappointment. This scenario will never occur. You must give this up. Your time here is almost over. Can't you enjoy what you do have and let the pipe-dream alone?"

"Never, I'm telling you that I know this dream is my destiny."

They looked into each other's eyes.

"Then, I'll help you search."

The next two weeks, they traveled all over Provence. Often, her friend would grab her shoulder and point to a man or child, but her dream man's eyes did not meet hers.

Gustus drove her to the home of Monet. They visited rustic vineyards, classy art studios, fields of lavender, and Van Gogh's sunflowers. Cezanne's mountain filled her art now, but her dream never showed. That lone mountain which filled the art of her favorite painter represented the Frenchman to her. He loomed over all of her thoughts and dreams. A large, intimidating mountain which felt impossible to climb. Meeting him had become her goal for such a long time. All of Savannah's dream places welcomed her but not the man. His hand never extended to hold hers. She and the Italian continued searching for him but to no avail.

Finally, Gustus sadly announced one evening that they should return to Portofino.

"I do realize the disappointment which you experience, but we are wasting precious time looking for your dream. Home calls to me; I must return, yes?" Savannah agreed. Two days later, the small, red Fiat left gorgeous Provence for the return to Portofino. The woman no longer spent time thinking of him. If it was destiny for them to meet, this must be the place. Obviously, Gustus was correct. Her dream man was only that, a dream.

Once again, they drove through small spells of rain showers with the top down. Finally, the red convertible slowly drove up the winding path by the villa. The couple happily walked into the welcoming arms of Annabella.

"Good grief, you were gone such a long time. It is wonderful to have you back home. Savannah, my cousin said something about the two of you were 'on a mission?' Was it a success?"

The American smiled dreamily, "Yes, it was a success. My mission is now over. Life calls to me. I have my wonderful life and **House** with which to look forward."

She hugged Annabella gently; she walked slowly to her room.

# THIRTY-EIGHT: GUSTUS FINDS HIM

Such a short time remained in her vacation. Still, it became impossible to loosen the strands of moroseness which pulled at her. Savannah went through the same five stages of grief which faces everyone when they suffer loss.
In the beginning, she experienced denial. She denied that the Frenchman could ever love her. Slowly, her acceptance of the possibility encouraged her dream to develop.
Sadly, she remembered when anger flooded her soul. Why would God not answer her prayer! Hadn't she accepted HIM? She believed that God placed the dream of love from this outstanding man in her. At one point in her life, she may have laughed off such thoughts. They would have been immediately put to rest. Now, she accepted that someone so unlovable as she may find joy in the arms of this extraordinary man.

Acceptance of the dream dissipated the previous anger. Instead, Savannah found herself bargaining with God.

"If you let me find him today, I will be a better person. I'll go to mass more often, and I'll tithe. Won't that please you? I'm going to be a devoted mother to the little girl and the best wife imaginable to him. Please, God, let me find them."

When that didn't happen, she resorted to depression. That was where she remained in the final days of her trip. Acceptance, the final stage, seemed unlikely. Instead, she would remain trapped in depression because her dream refused to materialize. What was wrong with God?

Savannah attempted to appear unchanged to the people in her life with whom she remained closest. It was easy to become a robot who laughed at the right times and smiled constantly. Inside, her heart broke. Gustus knew what she experienced. At one point in his life, he felt so different and unlovable that he considered suicide. Thanks to the help of a priest, those thoughts were dragged into the light while he discussed the unwanted state which seemed destined for him. The kind priest issued sound advice. The young man listened with interest and relief to the words of the priest. After seeking like-minded people, he found camaraderie with others who also felt the same emotions. Life became different for him, but there existed the possibility of happiness. Gustus realized that doom did not await him. He had the opportunity to find acceptance and love. His bright smile had beamed again. At that point, he decided that he would show acceptance to all of God's children. Who was he to judge? Hadn't Jesus taught us that in His short life? *Judge not so that you aren't judged?* Gustus now had many friends and a life which brought him happiness. It was not his desire to marry or appear like *normal* people.

One of the hardest things that involved accepting his status as a gay man was explaining it to his family. When Gustus sat for the most awkward meeting of his life before his Uncle Luca and Aunt Maria, he struggled to find the right words. Trying to explain that he was different went better than he expected with his Aunt Maria and her husband. The young man labeled as different eventually did find happiness. What more could he desire? His family still loved him and accepted him just as he was. Gustus did not search for a gay partner. Life provided contentment without such. His faith kept him rooted in peace with himself and his fellow man.

Savannah continued to paint and study her books of art. Opera thrilled her soul but not to the previous degree when she believed that she would be the wife and mother to these beautiful people. With deep remorse, she buried Melissa and the handsome Frenchman of her dreams.

Probably much as Gustus buried dreams of being married with children long ago. The two had much in common. No wonder that he seemed to understand her well.

Only five days remained in Portofino. The moroseness continued to grow. When she left this place, it would be over as far as her destiny. Angrily, she leveled dark red paint onto the canvas. The sunset that she painted looked like a fire instead of a peaceful painting. She stopped and stepped back from her work.

"This has to stop! Why can't I control my emotions? What a ridiculous situation I have created. Ugh!"

She shook with defiance.

Suddenly, Gustus ran breathlessly toward her.

"It is him! I have seen the beautiful Frenchman!"

"Gustus, this isn't funny. So what, you have a group of friends waiting to watch as I make a fool of myself? Where

exactly did you see the Frenchman and daughter?"
"There is no girl. The Frenchman is accompanied by a beautiful woman who appears to be French as well."
Savannah fell to a chair in tears.
"This is the worst possible thing. Now, my love must break my heart by parading a beautiful woman before me? Will my life never stop humiliating me? This is the final episode! He is no longer my dream."
Gustus pulled her roughly from the chair.
"You get up right now and fight. Have you ever fought for anything? Don't you see that if you give up, you will always wonder what may have happened? You have the opportunity to find your dream. I never did. Come right now before they leave. It looked like they were preparing to leave. Hurry!"
"Gustus, I can't. My legs are shaking, and I can barely breathe. Please understand. I'm not a fighter. Maybe I'm

Italian, you know, 'a lover, not a fighter.' Just let it go."

Gustus physically picked her up and threw her into the convertible. As she screamed and hit at him, he drove to the best restaurant on the beach. He pulled her resistantly from the car as he shoved her in front of him into the restaurant. Several passing men looked at them with concern. They almost intervened because it appeared that the Italian abused the woman but quickly Gustus shepherded her inside.

Together, they stood at the entrance by the hostess.

"That group of Frenchmen with dates are they still here?"

The tanned young woman with platinum hair smiled.

"Weren't they beautiful people? Some of the women were famous models. Maybe the men as well, if not, they should be. No, they just left. They were transported away in a limousine. I'm sorry."

The Italian looked at the American with shock.

"We barely missed them?"

Savannah stopped the tears and smiled. "I can handle it now because you see, it wasn't meant to be. Don't worry about me; I'll be fine."

Gustus smiled. He knew better. He had played the same game at one point in his life. It was difficult to bury a dream.

"Good because I'm starving. Can I buy you lunch? I think they are still serving."

Later in the day, depression left Savannah. Maybe the message from God was that the Frenchman and daughter were not her destiny! She would treasure them in her heart but not as hers.

Annabella listened to the emotional story from Gustus and Savannah later when they returned to the villa. She was the person who always offered support. Instead, she looked at Savannah with alarm.

"When you return to the States, you need to seek professional help. No one can recover from grief this quickly. You are back in denial. Please, I beg you to consult someone, or you may remain stuck there forever."

Savannah felt fine. Still, she agreed to the pleas of her friend. There was no reason to upset her.

Savannah retired early after an outstanding dinner from Annabella. Her dreams refused to obey her wishes. The Frenchman stood inside **House**. He loved the gracious home. Melissa ran down the halls and stroked the shiny, white walls. She seemed to understand the power which **House** possessed. Suddenly, someone was shaking the sleeping woman roughly.

"Savannah, wake up. He is here. The Frenchman wants to meet you. Hurry! His girlfriend is waiting at one of the bars on the beach. He can't tarry. Please run!"

Savannah looked around the room. Darkness enveloped it. Gustus stood over her.

"What do you mean, he is here? How can that be possible?"

"I saw him with his entourage of friends. I explained how badly you desired to meet with him. He understood and agreed to come. You must hurry."

"My make-up, I should dress, and look presentable."

"Savannah, I have never seen you look any lovelier. You don't need all of the make-up. You glow. Come, right now. Do you trust me? Then come."

She knew that they were making a terrible mistake but followed him down the stairs. As they walked outside in the garden, the man of her dreams turned toward her with a look of intenseness. His smile melted her. She felt ridiculous.

"It is you? Since we saw each other in New York, I have dreamed of you. I know this sounds absurd, but I need to talk with you." Those were his words.

Gustus pushed her toward the handsome man. She stumbled and almost fell but strong arms caught her. He pulled her into an embrace. Suddenly, his lips came forcibly upon hers. This treatment frightened her, but she did not recoil. He kissed her for the longest time. As he did, the roughness dissipated into the kiss of a lifetime. Her legs felt weak as her entire body trembled with desire for him. Savannah heard Gustus quietly walk away.

They sat in the chaise lounge which she shared mostly alone all of the past months. Their quiet laughter rose softly into the fragrant night. He held her hand just as in her dreams. The bond between them was instantaneous. Still, they agreed that this sudden closeness felt strange.

"What about your girlfriend? Shouldn't you return to her?"

"I completely forgot about them. I'm sure that my friends have left by now for a different spot. You are right; I need to go back. If they have left me, may I return to you? Let's sit right here and enjoy this entire night. I'm not sure where we are headed, but I know that nothing like this ever happened to me. I'm afraid to leave you. You may evaporate. Are you really here?" Savannah called for Gustus who walked sleepily out of the house. He drove her love away. She felt confident that the group had indeed left him by now. Faithfully, she waited for his return. Hours passed. Finally, the little red car glided up the hill. Gustus had been drinking.

"They are all nice. The Frenchman's girlfriend is lovely. You will like her." Savannah looked at him with disbelief. "Are you insane? I will **like** his girlfriend. Don't you get it? I want to **be** his girlfriend. How did he seem once he returned to her?"

"Fine. He looked jubilant. He kissed her a few times, and they mumbled what I suppose were little love comments."

Savannah stood. As she walked away, over her shoulder, she only said one word "traitor."

Hours passed the next morning as Gustus and Annabella waited for their guest to come downstairs. Finally, around lunchtime, Savannah entered the bright kitchen.

"Has he phoned?"

"No."

The American nodded sadly. "They are laughing *at* me. Do you realize that I would have slept with him? I wanted him that badly. This entire thing disgusts me. I'm sorry that I was rude to you, Gustus. You were caught up with belonging to the 'in the in-crowd.' I understand. No worries between us. I'm not hungry. Surprise me with dinner tonight, Annabella. By then, I will be starving."

She managed a small smile as she stepped into a sunny, hot day. Painting did not interest her. Nothing did. Her desire was returning to **House** as quickly as possible. Savannah sat in the chaise lounge which he enjoyed last night. He must think her an idiot.

Hot, uncomfortable hours passed without a breeze, but the woman remained glued to her chair. Her body felt broken. She ached. Maybe she was sick? A smile briefly kissed her lips. *Yes, I am love-sick and a fool.*

Lunchtime came and went, but Savannah ate little. Instead, she clutched to her remaining thread of him: The chaise lounge which he occupied last night. His memory burned with sharpness. The kiss felt real. How could he not have been sincere?

Savannah finally staggered inside from the heat. Gustus and Annabella watched her sadly.

"You need to drink water. If you don't, you may become dehydrated."

"Okay. Later. Nap."

Quietly, she climbed the stairs.

Suddenly, the roar of an Italian sports car shook everyone to life. The door chimes rang over and over. Had there been an accident? The interloper was demanding and anxious. Annabella ran to the door.

"Savannah, you must come down! I need to talk to you." The words were shouted by the Frenchman. He called to her from the foot of the stairs.

She smiled briefly but continued to climb the stairs again without answering him. He followed her. They entered her bedroom. When she turned, he grabbed her, and attempted to kiss her again.

"What is wrong with you? Do you think that I am so worthless that I will do anything just to be with you?"

He threw her onto the bed. Passion controlled both of them. They were unable to prevent their feelings. They made love gently with deep caring. Savannah shook her head. What was wrong with her? Again, she let him use her only to discard her later when he laughed with his beautiful friends about her vulnerability.

"Can you believe that anyone can be so desperate? Heck, I'll visit her later tonight. Maybe all of you want to accompany me? She doesn't seem to mind." They would all laugh uncontrollably.

Instead, he took her hands.

"Listen carefully to me. I do understand how you must feel, but I am not using you. Everything which I told you last night is true today and forever. The girl, whom Gustus met last night, is my fiancé. We have a wedding planned for early next year. After my time with you, I broke it off. Could I have gone back to her and explained about you so quickly? It required time. Even so, she was devastated. My friends all left with her. I probably lost my best friends forever, but I don't care. Just tell me that I did not make a mistake in my handling of this delicate arrangement. I didn't sleep at all last night. Instead, Tiffany and I discussed our life all evening. She cried and begged me not to do this. Here I am, if you still want me. Now, I realize that my relationship with her was a mistake." He hung his head briefly. Then, he turned with a questioning look.

The silence was the only thing which he heard. Moments ticked past. Finally, Savannah breathed deeply.

"I want you."

## THIRTY-NINE: WHAT'S NEXT?

Two months flew past. Savannah awakened early on a Tuesday morning and stretched luxuriantly as a cat often does. Happily, she looked around her new home. It was impossible being away from Léo. They had been a couple since that night when they realized that there was indeed something special between them.

The villa could not extend her time there any longer. A different person from Latin America had rented the space. Although it proved difficult saying, "Adieu" to Gustus and Annabella, the presence of Léo made it easier.

Now, she awakened each morning in a dreamy, little cottage looking directly at Cézanne's beloved mountain, Montagne Sainte-Victorie. This beautiful place overlooked Aix-en-Provence in the area where she and Gustus searched for the elusive Frenchman. Savannah experienced such joy and peace each day.

Every morning, Léo's soft kiss alerted her that it was time to begin their day. Together, they strolled his vineyards of mainly Grenache grapes. His red wines gained tremendous respect from all over the world. His miles of grapes were located nineteen miles north of Marseille in Provence-Alpes-Côte d'Azure. Together, they walked his vineyards daily. The weather there was perfect for raising healthy grapes. With over three thousand hours of sunshine annually plus an annual temperature of 58 degrees Fahrenheit, there was little to cause worry. The conditions prevented unwanted rot or vine disease. A delightful *cold mistral* regularly blew down the Rhone. That was the only concern; the wind often damaged the delicate vines. Plus often, there were violent storms in the spring and fall ushering in over thirty inches of annual

rainfall. Still, she and Léo enjoyed each day.
Her love introduced her to pottery. His property had a small cottage in the back with a potter's wheel. Since the area contained vast deposits of limestone, it was a natural pastime. Savannah already completed two lovely jars for **House**. One day, as she worked on her jars and he painted a large canvas of sailing scenes, she broached the subject dear to her.
"Leó, you were never married before?"
He looked startled as his black eyes stared at her.
"No, of course not. Don't you think that I would have mentioned something that important? Why? Have you?"
She realized how foolish she sounded.
"No, of course not, but there aren't any little white-haired girls belonging to you out there?"
He laughed good-naturedly.

"Well, only my niece, Claire. She is the love of my life, second only to you, of course."

He stopped and walked to the small galley in the cottage. He poured two large glasses of wine and motioned for her to join him by the fireplace. Already, the chilly mistral blew down the Rhone corridor. They cuddled together. Savannah couldn't wait until the colder weather would blow in their direction. She imagined large pots of delicious soups prepared by Léo's cook, Agathe. It amazed her how easily everyone welcomed her into the fold. Already, friends and Léo's family kidded them about marriage. They belonged together. Maybe it happened way too fast, but it happened.

"For quite a while, it has been my desire to broach this subject. I want you to meet Claire, but when you do, I must be sure that you are ready for us. You see, her parents died in a horrible skiing accident two years ago. Claire is only seven years old. She resides in a boarding school. There has already been tremendous pain and much change in her young life. She is my charge. My inadequacy as a parent stared at me from the first day that I picked her up from the hospital. Finally, I felt that it would be best for her to live in a boarding school. The school is located in the Swiss Alps. Tiffany did not want the responsibility of parenting with her busy schedule of modeling. Frankly, I can't cope with the constant demands either, so the school convinced me that they were the answer. Many students her age and younger call it home. She appears happy enough although she often talks about someday having a 'mommy.' She never met Tiffany because I knew that Claire would be disappointed. Children find out when they aren't wanted, you know."

Savannah's mind drifted to her childhood and the horror which she suffered at the hands of her parents. Yes, she understood well the sting of not being wanted. Leó's actions seemed to be the correct choice.

"I want you and Claire. Leó, I am asking you and Claire to marry me. Not now, I realize that it is way too soon but when you are sure. Come back with me to my home in Louisiana. You will love **House**."

He took her hand with a smile.

"I'm sure that I will but will she love me? You have told me the tales of that strange place. It makes me a little concerned to think of living there with all of the ghosts. Do you think she will welcome us? What about a little girl? Have children ever lived there?"

"This is the strange thing. The original owners, who also built **House**, were a French couple named Christophe and Claire Gautier. They had a little girl with white hair and azure eyes. Her name was, you guessed it, Claire."

Speechlessly, Léo looked into her eyes of dark honey.

"Are you making this up?"
Incredulously, she shook her head.
"Could anyone make this up? I promise. Will you come for a visit?"
"Yes, if you will you go with me to Claire's school? I want her to meet her new mother. If she is okay with this, we will take her out of that dreadful place and visit your home in New Orleans."
All day, they sat on the sofa before the roaring fire. Dreams and plans were made for a June wedding at **House.** Far away, as if she could hear the words, House smiled.
*Another wedding? I hope that it is as lovely as Clarissa's and Steven's wedding. Please come home, Savannah.*
The next week, the couple slowly drove across the Swiss Alps to the small school nestled in the branches of a high mountain.
Little Claire ran happily into the arms of Léo.
"Papa, you came early for me! It is not Christmas yet. Is it?"

Savannah looked into the bluest eyes she had ever seen. The innocence of a perfect alabaster complexion with a smattering of freckles across her turned-up nose would melt the heart of anyone. The woman looked silently at the little girl. Claire looked with interest at the woman. No one spoke for the longest time.

"Is this Tiffany? Your girlfriend? Do you want to be my mother?"

Léo squirmed uncomfortably.

"No, my darling, this lady is Savannah. She wanted to meet you."

"That's a funny name. What is Savannah? I have never heard it before."

Savannah explained to Claire about her beautiful home in New Orleans. Gently, she told about the wide-open areas which graced the marshes throughout the South.

"So, you see, where I live, this is a common name. I hope that you like it."

For the longest time, the child did not move. She stared as if frozen in the

same spot. Finally, she looked at her uncle.
"Do you like her Papa?"
"Yes, I do. I like her very much."
Claire smiled with tiny, pink lips at her future "MaMa."

## FORTY: *CLAIRE'S HOUSE*

*Claire's House* never looked as festive. Clarissa's wedding, which was held inside, sparkled with red and white roses. Savannah's wedding included the entire house. Flowers filled lavish containers. Big, bold sunflowers interspersed with lavender everywhere, both inside and out. Wonderful fragrances brushed the air. The wedding took place in the gardens by the blue waters of the lake. The reception which followed rocked the inside of the giant structure. Hundreds of guests proudly attended the lavish event.

All of the hookers who worked for Savannah as well as her friends with addiction problems arrived feeling important and wanted. No one was denied the joy of the moment. Claire told her husband everything about her past. Nothing was hidden.

Léo's friends and family came from France. They loved his new wife and were thrilled with **House.** It was a glorious time.

Little Claire strutted in her pink dress covered in frills and ruffles. Carefully, she dropped each of the pink rose petals in perfect timing. When too many fell, the girl would stop and pick them up. Then she continued happily. Léo groaned.

*Her OCD magnifies itself today.*

Next, Annabella walked behind Claire dressed in a taupe, sleeveless concoction. The color was the perfect accompaniment to the shining red hair now much longer and softer than when Savannah first met her.

Léo stood at the altar by his brother, Enzo. They both smiled from ear to ear. Finally, last but not least, Gustus walked Savannah down the aisle. The dress, which she chose, was a sleeveless cream gown of exquisite beauty. Intermittently stitched in the fabric glowed tiny jewels which reflected the late afternoon light. A full orchestra hailed her entrance.

**House** stood proudly over the happiest occasion of her existence.

Later, at the reception, each of the guests happily rocked on the marble foyer to the most beloved band from New Orleans. Cajun music dazzled the French guests.

"You know, I have been told that I have Cajun blood." The new husband smiled as he watched the musicians.

"What a coincidence, when the fiddle lets loose, everyone wants to be a Cajun." She smiled at her love. How did she ever win the heart of someone this special?

When she talked with the priest of the local parish before their marriage, he told her, "You didn't choose each other. God wanted you for Léo and him for you. Don't give yourself so much credit."

"Well, who chose me for Claire's mother and her for my beautiful, beloved daughter?"

"God," they said His name together.

Shortly after Léo, Savannah, and Claire arrived at **House** from France; Gustus had telephoned them.

"I miss you very much. Tears fill my eyes most days. How could I have known how hard this would be for me? Not having you in my life is too difficult. I miss you all so much."

The couple discussed his words. Quickly, they phoned him back and invited him to join their happy family. Now, they were indeed a complete package.

One day as Savannah and Léo lounged by the pool, they softly discussed their impetuous life.

"Dearest Savannah is there anything which would make you happier than you are right at this moment?"

"No, nothing could make me any more comfortable. Why? Anything more that you desire?"

"Honestly? For a while, I wished that we could have a son. When Gustus arrived, I decided that I couldn't take all of the

drama. I have adopted him as my son."
They laughed.

"Léo, he is older than you."

"I know, he is older but not nearly as wise. He is like a great big baby. I love him."

Claire's steps ran down the halls of **House**. Times now were reminiscent of earlier days when Babe delighted the structure with childhood noise. **House** watched all of the new days with interest and contentment.

Many years had passed in the shiny, white walls of this glorious place since the idea for her sprang in the mind of Christophe. Happy times as well as horribly sad ones. **House** cherished each of them. It was hard to remember all of the couples and families who walked across the threshold in the Louisiana bayou. Memories blurred with many passing years.

Léo fell in love with her when he first walked into the bold foyer. Now, the couple flew back and forth between his home in France and Savannah's here. Claire attended a local school in the New Orlean's area but happily lived at **House** instead of a boarding school. Gustus stayed by her side when the couple needed to leave but mostly, they all lived in **House** except during wine season when the couple were required to be present in France. It was a perfect life with two different lifestyles.

Nestled in a trunk in the attic, a group of documents lay tied together with a piece of twine. The family history of Christophe Gautier's Cajun family members waited for discovery. **House** knew that the couple could not take the news yet. It would seem too perfect or orchestrated by someone. When the time was right, Léo or Claire would discover the old documents.

"You know, I'm sure that I heard at some point something about my family having Cajun relatives in the States. Enzo remembers the same thing. We think that there was an Uncle Boyce or

some such name in our background. I think that there was someone with my same name in my past. Probably, I was named for him. Do you know anything about that original family? Wouldn't it be wonderful if I was related to them?"
"Now, Léo, you are pushing things a little far. What would the chances be that this could happen?"
"What would be the chances that we could find each other and have a life together? Miracles do happen, you know."
**House** trembled with emotion.
"Did you feel that? The house just shook. Didn't you feel it?"
"Right. So, you want me to believe that I caused the house to shake with my statements? I think that you are pushing it a little, my love."
They laughed contentedly.
"Well, I guess anything is possible when you live in **House!** Right?"

**House** shook more gently this time. Things had come full circle in *Claire's House.*

Write a review for Claire's House on Amazon and receive a free book. Please contact me if you would like to participate.

http://lindaheavnergerald.com

lilyhg@bellsouth.net

# LINDA'S NEX BOOK:

# ANNAPOLIS SUMMERS EXCERPT

My name is Anna Polis. I realize that you get it. My beautiful name strangely resembles the word Annapolis because my father is a couck. That word is from my Urban Dictionary. In other words, he is odd; he is brilliant but extremely strange. Don't get me wrong; I love my dad. He is funny, caring, adores my mother and me as well as brilliant. Please forgive me, I'm repeating myself. My story is one of love. It is a love for life. Much of the joy, which I experience now, is a gift from my father.
Herbert James Polis was born into a family of wealth and privilege. Private schools, the best in the world, shaped his outlook on life. Herbert identifies with the Republican Party, don't stop reading yet. He is a devout Christian and believer in the Constitution of the United States of America. Our bumper

sticker attests to the fact that we believe in the Pledge of Allegiance and the statement "Under God."

Herbert James Polis loves this great country of ours. He fought in two wars so that he can proclaim his beliefs. Proudly, I relate that Dad graduated from the United States Naval Institute. Hence, his love for that fair city which he calls, "The best damn city in the United States of America." In our family, you never leave off the phrase "of America."

Now, you're getting it, right? I, Anna Polis, am named after Annapolis. The place which my father loves most on this earth. I'm pretty safe avoiding uncomfortable moments about my name. Most people don't get the connection. Occasionally, some wise guy will scratch his head, "Your name sounds sort of like Annapolis. Did anyone ever tell you that?"

"Naw. Really? Like Annapolis? That is so cool! You are amazing!"

The idiot smiles and the awkward moment is forgotten.

Dad loves God, country, family, Annapolis, and sailing in that order. I'm grateful that he never named me Hinckley, Swan, or Hallberg-Rassey. Those vessels are three of his favorite sailing yachts. Each weekend and often during the week, when school vacations allowed, we moved aboard our boat in my childhood as dad did what he loved most, sailing.

Mom loved to cook in the tiny galley even though we had a spacious kitchen with our maid, Ellie, to do all of the work back home. They became different people once we boarded. Each of us knew our place.

The hierarchy developed years ago. Dad was the "Captain." All decisions were deferred to him. Mom was the "First Mate." She was also the cook for lunch only. After that one meal, we ate out for all others. Lesser problems were brought to her attention. I was the "Fifth Mate."

That title doesn't exist. You see, on the boat, I was nothing. It always seemed that I fell from my lofty status of "most important child in the world" to "nothing but a bother."

As an example, once, we suffered a gas leak on one of our boats. It took two days for Dad and Mom to have it checked out. In the meantime, I suffered from trouble breathing and severe headaches. The leak occurred in the forward berth where I resided. All of this because Dad didn't want to interrupt our plans to meet friends in St. Michaels. That was Herbert's second favorite city on earth. When they finally believed me about the leak, I had lost my appetite and almost threw-up. It is quite possible that I almost died, but Dad laughed it off. You see why I hate boats, sailing, and summers?

Each summer, we closed the house. Ellie must have loved her time alone. We had to check back once a few years ago. We never returned to the house once it closed for summer but that one time. She had her entire family from Guatemala living in our elegant mansion. They seemed to enjoy the pool a great deal as it filled with coke cans and chip bags. Our lovely home was a wreck. Dad almost had a heart attack. We were wealthy but frugal.

"We need to respect the things that I worked hard to obtain."

Great advice except Dad had a hefty trust fund established ages ago by one of our relatives who died before I was born. My Father never worked a full day in his life.

Most days, Herbert went to the "office." I never understood what he did there or why he went. Eventually, I figured that he got away from Mom and me for a few hours.

He enjoyed a golf game with his three best buddies and a long lunch at the club each week while at the "office."

Weekends, all activities went on "hold" even the golf games and office because we were always on the boat.
Summers of a "rich kid" are not that great, believe me. If you aren't involved in activities each moment of the day, you are not performing up to par. Your parents freak out that you might never be accepted into an Ivy League Institution, which is below death in their eyes.
That was the one good thing about sailing. No one demanded anything from me, unlike friends who were pushed to exhaustion. By the time school began, they were thankful for a break while I craved a challenge.
That was the one good thing about sailing. I sat alone in the corner of the boat with a good book or daydreamed. Now that I am an author, of mediocre reputation, I can point to those times as the beginning of my creative abilities. While Dad and Mom wowed their friends with the most skilled sailing

abilities among their elite group and the nicest boat, they left me alone to doodle on my sketches or write. I'm still publishing some of the stuff I wrote as a teenager. The old work is cool.

This senseless whiling away summer hours might sound great to you if you held a job at a fast food place all summer season in high school. Don't get me wrong, plenty of people suffered worse than me. Still, don't become too upset with the wealthier kids, we bore our piece of Hell. It isn't easy being nothing.

Weeks after school began and I was expected to be the nerd which I seemed destined to become, performing at A level created a dilemma for me. How does one go from being and doing nothing important to the expectation of Valedictorian? Not easy, I can tell you. I, Anna Polis, am an overweight girl with stringy dark brown hair, a bad complexion, and I wear glasses. I'm not exactly the "babe" in the string bikini which attracts the hunk on the next boat. In fact, when we pull into a marina, and the neighboring boat kids drift over to check out the most beautiful boat just arriving, I am not the beauty they expect. As I stumble out of the cabin, I usually hit my head and fall over my feet since my eyes hurt from the sun. Immediately, I return to replace my bottle thick lenses with my sort-of-attractive designer sunglasses which is a step-up for me. Still, as I emerge squinting into the sun with a broad smile hoping that someone like me is in the crowd, I am not amazed as the entire group walks away still talking to each other as if I was nothing. I am nothing. At least not until school begins and I assume my position as President of the Student Body and Editor of the school newspaper. When it comes to brains, I excel. Any other activity, I fall far behind everyone else.

All of the above information is true. I'm not trying to score sympathy here. What

I'm doing is setting the stage for my story. You may have trouble believing it. I still do.

# LINDA HEAVNER GERALD

Award-winning author, Linda Heavner Gerald, was recently voted by the public as one of Fifty Great Authors You Should be Reading. Linda also placed as a finalist in Novelunity, a competition for authors from all over the world.

Mrs. Gerald and her husband reside on the Forgotten Coast of Florida where they love to bike on trails by their home and enjoy walking on the most beautiful beaches in the world.

Linda writes each day. Her goal is to demonstrate that God loves all of us. No one is beyond his redemptive grace. A medical background allows this author to incorporate information into her writing with the hope that a reader, who is suffering from a similar problem, may consult a professional. She also is a world traveler who enjoys transporting her readers to distant places from the safety and convenience of their home. Linda feels that a good book should be more than just a good read; it should enlighten readers.

# CLAIRE'S HOUSE

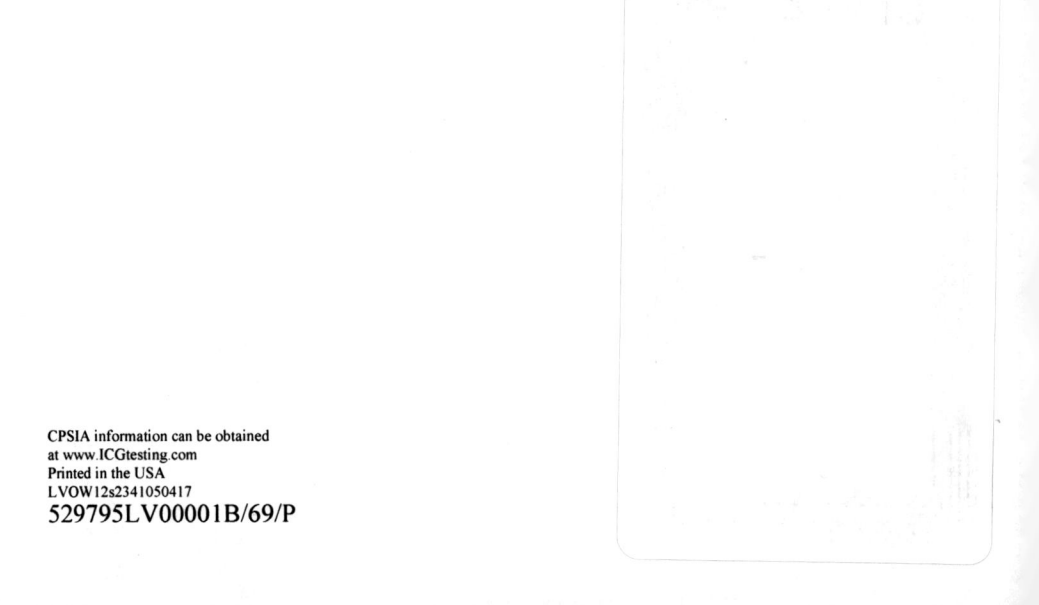

CPSIA information can be obtained
at www.ICGtesting.com
Printed in the USA
LVOW12s2341050417
529795LV00001B/69/P